the BLK love mixtape

brandon alexander williams,

editor-in-chief

Copyright © 2018 by Brandon A. Williams
All rights reserved. This book or any portion thereof may not be reproduced or used in any manner whatsoever without the expressed written permission of the publisher except for the use of brief quotations in a book review. For permission requests, write to the publisher addressed "Attn: Permissions Coordinator," at the email address below:
BrandonAlexanderWilliams@gmail.com

Printed in the United States of America First Printing, 2018

Cover Art Photography: Brian Freeman

for the Sistas.

For My... | *Malari SankofaWaters* -------- 10
Overu | *BLVCK SPVDE* -------- 11
Race Relations | *Harold Green* -------- 12
LoveLetHer | Brandon Alexander Williams -------- 14
She Is Magic | *Louis Conphliction* -------- 16
of African Descent | *13 of Nazareth* -------- 19
Only Girl | *George Jackson III* -------- 22
Love | *Rodzilla* -------- 24
Hair Poem | *Rage Almighty* -------- 27
Wasn't Looking | *Sam Trump* -------- 30
mother, Day | *LaRoyce Hawkins* -------- 32
Sun Spots | *Droopy, "The Broke Baller"* -------- 33
SpottieOttieDopaliscious | Big Boi -------- 38
Asking for a Friend | *A.D. Carson* -------- 39
Beautiful Black Woman | *J. Ivy* -------- 42
Blush | *Sean Ace* -------- 45
Black Queen | *John The Author* -------- 48
Dance With My Daughter | *Ace Metaphor* -------- 50
Jacuzzi | *Phenom* -------- 53
H.E.R. interlude | *Karega Bailey* -------- 55
Jack & Jill | *Dometi Pongo* -------- 56
Girls in the Hood | *Allah's Apprentice* -------- 58
Pure | *Black Ice* -------- 61
Natural Woman | *Corey Black* -------- 65
Love, Hate | *LaRoyce Hawkins* -------- 67
Starburst | *Jason Williams, The Poet* -------- 68
Black Love | *Tebe Zalango* -------- 70
Love Language | *Yaw* -------- 71
Beautiful | *Truth B. Told* -------- 72
Black Woman | *Mel Rob* -------- 74
Ma Mere n'a Jamais eu des ailes | *Pages Matam* -------- 77
Understanding | *Rewind* -------- 79
Black Women's Studies | *Brandon Alexander Williams* -------- 81
Atone | *Jaycee Cowan* -------- *85*
New Religion | *L.A. VanGogh* -------- 87
Three Queens and Apologies | *Cyrus Speaks* -------- 89
Ms. Natural | *Brown Audio* -------- *92*
Hibiscus | *Frankiem Nicoli* -------- 94
Lunar Admiration | *Brandon Douglas* -------- 96
Untitled-14 | *Kwabena Foli* -------- 99
Sweet Love | *R.O.E* -------- 101
For Trinity | *Tyson Langhorn* -------- 103
Black Woman | *Tebe Zalango* -------- 105

This Day | *Adán Bean* —107
All I Want | *Add-2* —109
Star | *Yusha Assad* —111
Helpless | *Malcolm-Jamal Warner* —113
Poet at a loss of words | *Karega Bailey* —117
Can I Love You? | *Tripp Fontane* —119
So Long | *Sam Trump* —121
Woman Can Stop the Rain | *Ques* —124
Future Wife | *Moementum* —127
For My Sistahs | *Just Flo* —129
I Prayed for You | *Orville The Poet* —130
My Sentiments | *Lee England Jr.* —132
A Laughing Matter | *Droopy, The Broke Baller* —134
Maybe Your Body is God | *Frankiem Nicoli* —137
Use Me Up | *El Thought* —139
Push | *Harold Branch* —142
Magic | *L.A. VanGogh* —144
RelaxHer | *Jus Cuz* —146
Mother Nature | *Limitless Soundz* —148
Savior | *Matt Simpson, The Man of Culture* —149
Ode to the Magic | *Pages Matam* —151
Girl | *Pugs Atomz* —152
Rose Gold | *Steve N. Clair* —153
Melanin | *The Boy Illinois* —154
Melanin | *T.L. Williams* —155
Love | *Yusha Assad* —157
The Art Institute | *Que Billah* —159
Gift | *Rashad Tha Poet* —160
Letters to Sister Betty: a haiku | *Daunte Henderson* —162
Dreamers | *Dion Jetson* —163
Sistuh Girl | *Keith "Keboi" Rodgers* —164
BodyPositivity | *BrandonAlexanderWilliams* —167
She in Her | *Zeaux Indigeaux* —169
24 Questions: A Handwritten Letter to Peach | *Dexter* —172
Adam's Rib | *Chris Wiley* —174
Myth | *Kwabena Foli* —178
Points | *Daunte Henderson* —179
She's a Blessing | *Drunken Monkeee* —180
Don't You Know | *Chris James* —182
B-E-A-U-T-I-F-U-L Spell | *Toni Mono* —184
Untitled (for Candy, 2) | *Billy Tuggle* —186
A Black One | *Kwabena Nixon* —187
Meant | *King Gandy* —189

for Myles, DaMarco, Stevie, Stafi, Pooh, Cameron, Alexander, Benjamin, Jordan and King Joseph:

You have value.
You are not disposable.
May you always cultivate safe spaces for BLK women.

FOREWORD

A mentor once told me to
"…create what you wish you had when you were younger."

This is one of those things.

While preparing to DJ a "woman's appreciation" event for the Zetas of Mu Delta a few years ago, I was told that I must play a bunch of songs that are uplifting for BLK women. I'd been DJing for about a decade so I already had a few joints in mind. The more I researched, I noticed parallels with the content and the era. Most R&B songs between the 1990s and 2000s that I found by men shared a common narrative with sexual undertones, the remainder were joints specifically for mothers or daughters. There were very few directed towards women that weren't sexual. And in those, they almost always contained apologies. "Baby forgive me..." Art imitates life. Hold that thought. Most songs that I found created by women shared a common narrative of heartbreak. A large amount were forgiving towards men.. "I love you even though..."

This revelation made me sad. I thought to myself, if I was a foreigner and I was given the top R&B albums of all time, I might walk away thinking "the BLK woman keeps getting her heart broken by the BLK man, but she still loves him" and "the BLK man adores his mother and daughter, but other than that, he's trying to have sex." This large void of art that uplifts BLK women is exactly why I created the BLK love mixtape. Let this serve as a recipe book. 86 different recipes of how to love a BLK woman accurately. I desire for BLK boys to identify love based on these examples given by the 60-something BLK men who've contributed to this book. I hope that they'll look at the photos in the biography section and see their reflection in the men that they look like and/or will look like one day. I pray that every BLK woman that reads or hears these words gets healing from them.

Let these poems be medicine.

This is a historical matter of record where BLK men declare, profess and cultivate their love for the BLK woman.

For maximum experience:

1. Read one piece silently.
2. Read the same piece aloud.
3. Scan the QR code on the page and listen to the audio of the author delivering the piece.
4. Share this with a friend and have a conversation.

For My… | *Malari SankofaWaters*

For my super hero on stilts
My looks could kill shotgun sassy sunshine
Hearts
Wrapped in steel
Not cause you hard but cause you a hard lover
One baaaaaaaad mutha
But bad as in good
Sure as you needed no words to be understood
Naughty by natural
You make titans of the tender headed
To the women that made a man out of me
Thank you

Overu | *BLVCKSPVDE*

Tears will fall again for you, for you
And hearts will melt again over you over you
Flowers will bloom in cold shaded places for you, for you
and I'll remember to always say your name
how could I forget you
and I remember it was my heart to blame for falling for you
so may the memory of you stay with me onto the other side

The sky and moon and stars
Are over you, but not me, not me who's over you…

Race Relations | *Harold Green*

no woman outside my race has ever been into me
and not because I deem us enemies
I have never pursued
and not because of vanity
I've found beauty in all shades

I think it has to do with connection
I'm pretty steadfast when it comes to connection

I need you to hug me
Like you know what it feels like to be snatched from me
Or like we both tried our best
Pressed through being oppressed
And your breast pressed against my chest
might be the best thing we have left
I need you to look me in my eyes
like you've seen what has happened and know what may come
But still you wont forget this place
As small as a pupil
But as big as we make it
Let's make it one to remember
I want you to remember me
Like when I leave here you know it's a chance I may not come back
And although that's a risk we might take
Remember ours is multiplied by the property of black
Rub my head
as if you know how it must've swelled after being propelled
by gallons of rushing water into unforgiving brick walls
kiss me like we've made it this far
off the strength of these wrists
every time they knocked us down
we lift us up
let me hold you
like I had to watch you go through

things I had no control over
and this is my sorry
this is my circumference of empathy

let me caress your head
just to make them jealous
just because they're not allowed to
and because I know how unique it is
I know it makes you rare
I know (like you) it requires special care

Let me talk to you
Like I'm trying to help you forget everyone who did it wrong

Let me kiss you
As if we're both seeking justice and found our answers
right here
in this moment, simultaneously
I don't know if I can find that answer on other lips
I don't know
I haven't tried
But this makes sense
The world has forged our bond even tighter
We defy stereotypes within our existence
Within your presence, I feel gifted
And you feel different

Maybe they've never been into me

Because I was too
into you.

LoveLetHer | *Brandon Alexander Williams*

dear future wife
this is a love letter
written in a colonized tongue,
and it's not a confession
nor is it stressing
to apologize all that I've done

please overstand that
there's a higher you
if you choose me
I won't acquire you
listen closely
I'll admire you
I don't need you
I desire you

need is operating from deficit
desire is more adjacent and evident
of free will and Love making indefinite
love has been always a predicate

never a noun
only a verb
ever endowed
only superb
delivered with passion
love is
it just is
it just be
living in action

so if I'm just existing and passive
somebody pinch me and give me a massive
make up wake up calllike hey young GODbody
pick ya face up dog

makeup wake up call
like when MAC cosmetics got the voicemail and new wind
"Fenty got 72M's!"
tell me what are you gonna do when
the sistas that are MUA's
don't re-up when they run out
of your product and don't care bout
new stuff and don't come out

I digress
this is my weakness
and strength also, critical thinking
I flex often lifting a thesis
reshaping, listen and reading
you can catch me Mentally feeding
what's between my temples with geek and
air quote nerdy lyrical things and
spiritual breathing, and freedom
fam this is intriguing

to what I mean
know what I mean?
I'm meaning to say
I mean what I say
it's verbatim
explicit language
spoken word
no absurd
overheard
regurgitation

only scholarly
determining all I see
serving with honesty
deserving anomaly
one of a kind and
'Rega say
me no crazy
divine synchronicity
perfect timing

She Is Magic | *Louis Conphliction*

she so amazing
she like, looking at the sun blazing
you focus too long and your sight will be gone
her glow is just that strong
feast your eyes on the Queen
soon you will be enchanted
got me so enthralled, at times I can't stand

she magic
look at her over there, looking like sustenance
smelling like nourishment
just as sweet as she wanna be
but you better believe a rose has thorns for protection
she feels like still water at midnight, casting the moon's reflection
she is perplexing and confusing
humbling and eluding

she life
nothing as valuable as her will be had easily
she is knowledge and wisdom
spirit and emotion
always providing another step towards understanding

her hips sway like leaves when the trees are dancing
you know there is life there
she is two parts mermaid, one part pixie
nice with the magic wand
and as down to earth as dirt
down to earth like grilled cheese and top ramen
sorceress and shaman, I promise Mama got it
and even when she don't, she do
so in-tune
not many can do what she do
she can hypnotize you like mothers do

kiss your boo boo and the pain is gone
things change when she speaks it
get your heart moving just from hearing her say
"baby you can do it!"
she is dream-instiller

universe-wielder
family builder, all while some tear her down
her crown never falls off
even when she is knocked around, her head remains unbowed
with poker face strong
you won't get the last laugh
she is gifted
shape shifter
watch her move through different systems
she goes from teacher to absolute diva in a second
those that come against her, learn their lesson

she is magic
how else could she survive it all
sexism, rape, and degradation and still flawless
she renegade
she lawless
it doesn't make sense how much she loves

heart as big as the ocean her ancestors were brought over on
feet and toes fortified like cornrows and
back as strong as her fro when she lets it grow
something phenomenal happens when she natural

arms strong from uplifting her tribe
fingers equipped to make potions and stir miracles in the kitchen
feast fixed from minimum and will always leave you full from her giving
she is native
she is fashion statement
my inspiration
creative and creation align with her
she's a mythical being, that every story uttered, held some truth
she stay strong through the abuse
she stays strong through the abuse.
Ain't that magical?

how she stays fabulous in the face of tragedy

surpassing the miserable
even when she is treated invisible she is leading the pack

always radiant because some things just don't crack
like her faith

when her family is systematically being taken away
she finds a way to remain unchanged
all while evolving, she foundation
she anomaly
like the sun shining
there is living light in her skin
she was there in the beginning and will be there in the end
if you're still unsure, I will remind you again
she is magic.

# of African Descent | *13 of Nazareth*

dear Woman of African descent
spread across the continents
by knowledge and ignorance
you may currently find yourself
unable to find yourself wholly
represented in global pop culture

you may currently find yourself
thinking this inability to find yourself
is an implication that you are lost

you may currently find yourself
wondering that if you are lost
why has no one come searching?

I struggle to deliver you
answers that are neither
exaggerated nor dismissive
answers that acknowledge you
without defining you in a man's word
or confining you to a man's world
of ideological boundaries made
to make me feel more comfortable
being a man

it is easy for me to honor you
it is hard for me to not conquer you
when all my lessons teach dominance
as a prerequisite for sharing your time

even now, I struggle to not make this about me
taking the form of a hero who writes
rescue letters to a woman who is free
but only needs to remember
a woman represented in pieces
because the whole of her will not fit

into pop culture without breaking
the mold made to increase sales

a woman who sees how well
the pieces of her are accepted
by the mass and attempts to shrink
but remains rejected by the middleman
who is absolutely in love with her
but must deny the public access
to the source of his revenue stream

and truth is best hidden in plain sight
you are no more lost
and no less valuable than oxygen
is to a people who breathe oxygen
you are also no less accessible
and therefore you are unnoticed
unless you are missing

a woman whose body travels the globe
minus the presence of her mind or soul
the past century alone
bares witness to your curves
moving from freak show to side show
from opening act to main attraction

those who considered you
to be the species of a lesser class
were simultaneously risking cancer
to temporarily adorn your tan and now
their daughters spend college tuition
to acquire your lips, your hips and
other voluptuous accoutrements

your body has been a hot commodity
in which the whole planet has invested
you have both recognized and capitalized
but with all of the revenue generated
your body is your least valuable asset

your journey through history is history
man went back in time as far he could
in efforts to find himself and found you

you are the first chapter of humanity
you are what the world has in common
and each morning that I awake
from the writing of this verse forward
I will require myself to do two things

first, I will thank God for my life
and second, I will thank you
sincerely,
a Man of African Descent
who requires you to know
and be powerful

Only Girl | *George Jackson III*

you're the only girl in this world for me
you're the only love that this heart can feel
and I've known it from the moment that we met,
but I was scared to let you know just how I felt
you're the only girl in this world for me

it's like violins are playing,
it feels like I'm in heaven
when I'm staring in your brown eyes
It don't matter bout the weather,
in the middle of December it still feels like the summertime

Girl, my heart is on a tether for you
I'll be here forever
even if you never make a dime
I don't care about your money,
I just want you, Honey,
you get sweeter as the days go by

If I could go into the future,
I'd come back and bring you proof
that it is you who shares my life
and I'd do anything I have to
just to get my better half to
never have to ever ask me twice

I would even walk through fire
with a lion and a tiger
right behind me
just to see you smile

you're the only girl in this world for me
you're the only love that this heart can feel
baby, yeah yeah yeah

you're the only girl in this world for me
~~you're the only girl in this world for me~~
~~you're the only girl in this world ...~~

—

Oh,
this is some kind of beautiful
feeling that's new to me
but I'm gon' give it my all
I'm addicted to loving you,
feeling so wonderful,
oooh, I just can't get enough

got me all in my feelings, Baby
I miss you the minute you leave my space
I just want to be near you,
nothing can compare to
this beautiful music we make

feeling up on my luck,
I'll give you the best of me,
place all your bets on this love
we can beat all the odds,
keep believing that God
is the reason that we'll overcome

any issue and every fear
let His love be the tissue that dries our tears
you'll be safe in my arms,
I'll hold you forever
so close to my heart

Love | *Rodzilla*

summa dat Marvin Gaye, *Sanctified* love
Granny died a month after her husband love
"She ain't really part of my family, she my play cousin" love
parents stayed together love
had tough times, stuck it out, now it's *mo' better* love
no pre-nup love
"shut the fuck up talkin' bout my love!" love
that ignant, blind love
that make ya sleep good love
that talk it out til' you understood love
that make me an insomniac thinkin' bout love
hot, sweaty love
un-protected, committed monogamous love
a diseased-free love
friends who grew into a love
not no thug love
give a nigga a hug love
no homo, not on the down-low love
out in the open, holding hands in the mall love
large and small love
not no priest fucking boys at mass love
not with her just cause she got ass love
introduce ya to my mama love
find 2Pac, B.I.G. killer, fuck Osama love
carnival cruise to the Bahamas love
fix ya pancakes wit the Aunt Jemima love
"I'll eat yo spaghetti!" love
I'll help your bad ass two-year-old get ready love
we goin' steady, love
we ain't just talkin' love
we for real walkin' love
not no lust masking itself as love, love
summa dat Mary J. Blige, *What's the 411?* real love
daddies taking care of they kids love

forgiving the foul shit you did love
that forever ever love
meet ya in heaven, love
before you come over, bring me a swisher from 7/11, love
that revolutionary love
that courageous love
not no abusive subjugated love
not no misogynistic, pimpin' love
but not no simpin' trickin' love
some equal love
summa dat Martin Luther King Jr. non-violent love
but I'll pull a gun and shoot that bitch to triumph love
midget with a giant love
summa dat black on black love
that Afrikan love
diaspora united love
and intelligent love
not a "I love white Jesus" love
not a "I love New York", minstrel show love
a Nas, Mos Def flow love
a superstitious love
we celebrate Kwanzaa 'round chea, fuck Christmas love
a realistic love
a "I'll cook for you," love
"but you gotta wash them dishes!" love
that Big Mama beat yo' ass love
"I love you even though you short on cash" love
"I got you" love
but don't take advantage of me love
not no groupie love
ride in my hoopty love
if that bitch break down, push with me love
ride the bus with me, don't forget yo transfer love
don't be stupid for me love
not no compromising your character for a love
that ain't love
that's self hate.
no argument, more like a debate love
a make me better love
a *Delirious*, red leather love
a Bill Cosby coogi sweater love
a refined Claire Huxtable love
a holistic love

not a sadistic fetish love
I ain't tryna piss on ya love
not no just a fling love
a "I'll risk everything" love
push me on the swing love
help me with my bad habits love
a real dream, you can help me grab it love
"let's fuck like rabbits!" love

and raise our kids
with the same love

my Mama raised me with.

that's that real shit.

Hair Poem | *Rage Almighty*

I spent most of today
trying to flush yesterday's alcohol out of my body
because…
the turn up last night was real

so I'm standing in line at Starbucks
buying my expensive ass coffee
and this woman
had a stupid ass grin
on her stupid ass face
I already knew exactly what she wanted
I knew exactly what was going to happen next
she maneuvered that decrepit hole at the bottom of her face
to ask me,
"Can I touch your hair?"

now keep in mind,
she was already touching my hair
while she was asking me if she could touch my hair
and I'm not going to say what race she was
'cause race has nothing to do with this poem (she was white)
and then she said,
"Oh my goodness, it doesn't feel dry at all!"

Listen…
no my hair isn't dry or unkempt
and contrary to your belief, it smells amazing.
I'm Black.
Us Black folk have hair of wool
skin of bronze
eyes like fire of flame
and these brass feet
will Sparta kick you in the chest
if you ever touch my GODliness
without my permission.
you cannot touch my hair, because

I am not your pet
or a specimen at a zoo
Venus Hottentot told me to tell you "…or naw!"
I never sent invitations to your curiosity.
your hands are dirty.
don't touch me with your backhanded compliments.
my history begins in my roots.

I let my culture drape my crown
while the tips of my lineage rest on my shoulders
there are strands of stories scripted at the top of my back
and no,
you can't manhandle my Mother's narrative
I'm protective of my temple
that's why I keep my birthright
I got tired of people stealing my culture
so I loc'd my hair
so you can't get inside of it
you can't touch my hair
I'm still cleaning your ancestors' fingerprints off it

this is not just our hair
this is our heritage
a representation of who we are
we are black
we are adaptable
we were designed with thick skin to safeguard our hearts
and sharp tongues to cut your throat

don't touch my hair
unless you know each strand by its name
this is Henrietta,
this is Assata,
this is Harriet,
this is Marley,
this is Kendrick,
this is Cole,
this is Blu Ivy,

all of it is Africa,
there's a crescent continent
from my spine to the top of my scalp
so I wear my hair like a sycamore fig

waving from the banks of a middle passage
don't forget where you came from
and don't forget where you're going
and don't forget the women
who twist,
who cut,
who primp,
who weave,
who loc,
the women who sleep uncomfortably
and sit in the same spot for hours just to get they head right
for nobody else but themselves
and their family

myself,
and my family
is not a sideshow
or to be fondled in the middle of Starbucks, while I'm hung over

So, no, Cruella deVille,
you can not touch my hair
wit'cho rude ass…

Wasn't Looking | *Sam Trump*

One look in your eyes
sets me straight for a day
one touch satisfies
simply makes me okay
your smile is sunshine
breaks clouds on rainy days
every day is just fine
and you made it this way

I wasn't looking for love
but I found it

I mean
I would look for anything, but love
and I found it, found you

your presence fills me up
satisfaction in your touch
contentment in your love

you're an angel
you're the epitome of great
and I just gotta say; you take the cake
sock it to me
you german chocolate
warm cinnamon coffee
you give me 7Up
even in an off week
the mold of a bundt
cause you touch softly

zest of a lemon
the flavor's in your skin
sexy red velvet

lipstick on your grin

expensive taste
you're made from 24 carrots
and you're so sweet, save for me the big piece
your curves and proportion matches

your words hit my sense of smell,
it serves me well
like I can tell
there's five minutes left

best warm
but that's normal
cause you've been warm forever
warm since the day you were born
like right out the oven
since you were delivered

a cake to celebrate us
wedding with the layers
cause we're constantly building

I wasn't looking for love
but I found it

I mean
I would look for anything, but love
and I found it, I found you

your presence fills me up
satisfaction in your touch
contentment in your love

mother, Day | *LaRoyce Hawkins*

I wonder if Day is the mother of Night
and the Sun rises when the Moon is tucked in tight
and the stars light the skies
and harmonize sweet lullabies
but Night cries
cause he wants to play with the fireflies
so, mother Day reads Night this bedtime story
about the "Little Engine That Could"
cause…
that's his favorite.

and as she reads each word, letter by letter
Night calms down and slowly feels better and better
until his eyes become far too heavy to hold, so
finally they close…
and night seems to be asleep

so mother Day just enjoys this brief moment of relief..
puts behind her, the long hours she clocked in for the week
tries to sneak out and turns off the light,
but all of the sudden, Night
re-opens his eyes
and realizes that his Day has just gone by,
so he cries
"Mama, could you please, just stay with me…
cause I'm scared of the dark."

and mother Day stares at Night in the eyes and sighs
and says "Son, go to sleep…and be a good Night..
there is no such thing as Darkness.
only the absence of Light…
sleep tight."

Sun Spots / *Droopy, "The Broke Baller"*

Sun Spots
I see you
Well, at least as much as anyone can see the sun
Orblike over these squares on this chess board called Brookland
A queen
Rendering me a rook, man
I am sideways
You don't see God every day
Or maybe you do and just never knew
So every now and then God sends a reminder your way
Well if remembering is this good, I can't wait to forget again
Locks the color of earth
Full length skirt
Hips switching like Hillary Clinton's political positions
Work, work, work, work, work
Walk like Rihanna
You ARE The Wanted
And I'm usually rather reserved
Preferring to engage when some rapport is already unearthed
So inundated with tales of rampant street harassment that I rarely speak for fear of being perceived a ratchet
So focused on being a "good Samaritan" that I fear I've gotten bad at casual interaction
But as Tony M said in my favorite Prince song:
"I'd gladly change my state of mind for that behind
['Cause] I bet if you threw that ass in the air, it would turn to sunshine
You sexy mother . . ."
. . But I digress
In all seriousness
Maybe we were meant for each other
In Brida, Paulo Coelho spoke of seeing a glow
over your soul mate's shoulder
So what must it mean if your glow is so thorough
That I can't even see over your shoulder?
I mean, sister, you are Badu-ing it
And I wants me a window seat
You got hot-sauce-in-your-bag swag

And I'm a New Orleans boy, so I likes me some spice when I eat
So allow me to defy my default
Introduce myself as Droop Banner
And ask if I could be the gamma in your She-Hulk
And then…
And then the sun opened her mouth…
And in an instant, it was as if God switched to some sick sadistic misspelling misfit
And capitalized the G.O.P. in my Goapele
I've never seen a more flawless face
Making more flawed statements
Amel Larrieux with a fascist facelift
Erykah Badu with her head wrap removed revealing a swastika tattoo
You looked like Elle Varner
And talked like Ann Coulter
You were the Apollonia of my eye
But I was the one getting trashed
You broke me
The heart was an afterthought
When you declared that black people have deplorable grammar
I judo chopped your cynical sneer
With a smile the politeness of which was almost as misplaced as your generalized judgmentality
And I thought to myself: "Ain't dis about a bitch?"
When you posited that black people carried zero critical context in their combative, divisive arguments
I stared at the glitter garnish
Around those gorgeous God-given soul holes above your nose
And thought to myself:
"I know you are, but what am I?"
When you chattered
That Black Lives Matter
Was no more than a groundless
Unfounded
Disorganized
And ludicrous
Pseudo-movement
Which would only
If anything
Make "matters" worse
I said:
"But . . "
To which you sucked your teeth

And uttered brief:
"Black people love them some but(t)s."
To which I replied:
"Nothing worth debating is simple."
To which you actually
Paused
Reflected
And agreed with me.
This would be the first
And last
Such occurrence.
When you said that the young generation was a lost cause
I knew that my designs on you were too
And Andre 3000's words rang true
When he hath sayeth:
"Is every nigga with dreads for the cause?
Is every nigga with golds for the fall?
Naw."
When you defended Donald Trump,
Saying he couldn't be racist
Because your girlfriend worked in one of his restaurants
and she was as black as the strap of my backpack
I felt like Harriet Tubman with my cross hairs trained on my own spouse
Knowing if I let that trigger go
That nigger would be the first one to make that whistle blow
When you said that black women
Couldn't keep black men
Because black women had terrible attitudes
My stuck smile became a sad one
Due as much to the statement
As to the irony it was laced with
Because, black woman,
You have just lost me
Because of your terrible attitude.
When you charged that every black woman from 18 to 25 should be sterilized
Your words were the vasectomy of me
As before my eyes my Beyoncé became Becky With The Good Hair
Getting me drunk in love
Off her Willie Lynchburg Lemonade.
And as I bear witness to this beautiful face spewing disgrace
I realize I've never seen a lovelier self-hate

I'm reminded of my youthful crush on Stacey Dash
It was so much easier when I was Clueless
But I can't do this
Because if I ever brought you home to my family, they would lose it
And so I go from Elle Varner
To Ellie Goulding
Because "I could have really liked you…
…and my heart don't understand it."
My dear nadir
With the diabolical deliciousness of the death sentences which drip
From your luscious apoca-lips
You kill me
And death becomes me
You pretty little Hitler
Every devastating decibel of your dictatorial doctrine
Dragging me deeper into the dank depths of your dogmatic dungeon
A veritable gas chamber
swamping my poor pores
with the hot air of your harsh hubris
and the humidity of my humility
Arsenic and old lace with an emphasis on "cynic"
Miss Information
You slay
You marvelously monstrous mashup
of Conya Doss
and Condoleezza Rice
With the face of Hillary from Fresh Prince
and the ideas of Uncle Ruckus from The Boondocks
My black sister
You beautiful fool
I cannot bring myself to hate you

To paraphrase the poet Jenny V:
You're much better at it than me
All that I can do is work
Work
Work
Work
Work
to be the best black man I can

And try to create hope where you see holocaust
And the next time I see you float your orb

to rest across this urban board of chess
I will switch from rook to king and let the queen come to me
Hopefully not so blinded by what I preconceive
That I can't even look over your shoulder
to see if there's anything there for me.

SpottieOttieDopaliscious | *Big Boi*

Yes, when I
first met my SpottieOttieDopalicious Angel
I can remember that damn thing like yesterday
the way she moved reminded me of a brown stallion horse
with skates on, ya know
smooth like a hot comb on nappy ass hair
as I walked up on her and was almost paralyzed
her neck was smelling sweeter than a plate of yams with extra syrup
eyes beaming like four karats apiece just blindin' a nigga
felt like I chiefed a whole O of that Presidential
my heart was beating so damn fast
never knowing this moment would bring another
life into this world

funny how shit come together sometimes, ya dig
one moment you frequent the booty clubs
and the next four years
you and somebody's daughter raisin' y'all own young'n
now that's a beautiful thang
that's if you're on top of your game
and man enough to handle real life situations, that is

can't gamble feeding baby on that dope money
might not always be sufficient
but the United Parcel Service
and the people at the post office didn't call you back
because you had cloudy piss
so now you back in the trap
just that,
trapped

go on and marinate on that for a minute…

Asking for a Friend | *A.D. Carson*

Try this one out.

I probably should
start by saying that—

that I don't
ordinarily do this kind of thing.

And for good reason.

But

dig.

I have, uh …

I've never been so
delusional that I believed my
heart would skip or
I'd lose command of my voice and
instincts.

But I was born with a murmur,
a slight stutter
and a lisp, so

those are fairly familiar phenomena I've practiced ignoring
or perfected working around my entire life.

What I want
doesn't require stars falling from the sky
or a profound understanding of
neurochemical triggers or being delivered from the sort of solitude
relegating one to a place only one other person would ever understand.

Shit—
what I want
may not even be poetic.

I want,

at its very simplest,

friendship.

The kind of friendship you don't die from not having, but
you can't fully live without experiencing.

The kind that—
that you cherish like
like memories
of a future
too dope to yet imagine, so
you can only dream—
you can only hope to dream
or déjà vu your way through the time until it's realer and clearer
than the magnificent mirage you so hopefully looked forward to.

The kind where
hands and doors held count

as much as
talking and listening,
laughing and crying,
living and loving,
kissing and hugging,
and all that other corny shit
I hardly ever write or talk about.

And that's probably one of my many, many, many flaws,
but believe me,
when I think it I feel it,
and when I feel it I say it, so
there's no way you're gonna be her
and not hear about it.

I'm tempted to say there's no way you're going to be her
and not change me, but
I hesitate because I know, at least in that way,
I'm already that way,

but in others, I'm open to
learning

and knowing
and relearning and knowing more
of the everything you might want,
hope, think
or unintentionally teach,

and I'm a willing,
lifelong learner, leader and
liker of cool shit and clichés I deny I like out loud, but

practice in private like a child

trying to impress.

So, uh…can we be friends?

Beautiful Black Woman | J. Ivy

In a dream is where she was first seen,
Golden brown,
Heaven-sent,
Hints of honey,
Beautiful chocolate,
Caramel,
Healing falling from her lips,
Mahogany dripped,
Like slices of silk cut from the deepest abyss,
Her light is lit like she was dipped in the sun,
She's the one,
Her dark matter matters,
Because she's God's gift,
Angelic,
Heaven's in-
Her melanin,
Her black skin feels like a sun-ray,
Warm,
Holy like Sunday,
I prayed to God that I would find one like you one day,
Her beauty struck me like a drunken driver,
Driving the wrong way down a one way,
She's so fly she could model any runway,
I couldn't catwalk nor run-way,
This is no accident,
With her my purpose is fine tuned,
Her spirit touched me before she entered the room,
I feel her,
It's as if my soul willed her,
She's magnetic,
Electric,
She carries the essence of God in every step,
She's a direct connect to the beginning,

With her there is no world ending,
Because she's close to the source,
The root and the seed,
A power source,
A force who has the power to change course,
And carry worlds in her womb,
Tell you how to get to the moon…
And her figure ain't hidden,
Body of a goddess is a given,
Her shape,
Sexy landscape is to be admired and adored,
Explored with respect,
Peace is felt whenever her aura is met,
She's magical,
A miracle,
Her spirit is a spiritual,
A gospel that's meant to be sung and praised,
Look at the the villages she's raised,
In small towns and city blocks,
Where opportunity is often blocked,
But everyday she manages to find a way to stop oppression,
Survive and shine,
I'm honored and humbled to call you mine,
It would be a crime not to love you completely,
Repeatedly,
Daily,
The queen and her crown,
I know who you are,
Your worth is profound,
She's the foundation of mankind,
Don't step on this landmine,
Cause her power is explosive,
Like when two stars collide,
The perfect picture is forever in motion,
Because she's beyond wise,
Stories of her pain is found in the tears she's cried,
But her joy doesn't escape her
Her hope takes her to the next breath,
The next example of her wealth,
Her astonishing feats,
She's the one you take home for Moms to meet,
Damn, I wish my Grandma could have met you,

And bared witness to the intuitive phenomenon that only you can bring true,

Beautiful Black Woman,
She would have loved you,
The same way,
That I do…

Blush | *Sean Ace*

Before I had a love for the birds
I used to dribble the rock
and handle the words
study Tribe and Camp Lo
and write a verse
if I ain't good as common or Jay,
I'm on the verge

That's 8th grade how I'm feelin
until this woman walked in
looking like a million

I remember telling Daniel
and Steve and DeShaun
when she walked in the room
"I can't eat."

My appetite leaves
sometimes I can't breathe
if the CPR giver ain't she
let me be

Only a few others like that
in high school
who is the model with the body
and the nice shoes?
looking like a young Robin Givens
I heard she got a man
but, I'm 'bout robbing, stealing

I talk a lot of mess to be blushing
but, if I get the look
I bet you I'm saying something
Remember letters, would you date me?
Check the box, that's yes, no or maybe?

some changed
as grown men and ladies
But you kept the charm
to make me blush baby

you got the charm
to make me blush crazy
you kept the charm
to make me blush baby
I got the charm
to make you blush? maybe.
~~(you got the, woooo to make me, uh!)~~

Damn,
it didn't work with the past ones
it's all good, cause I knew
they weren't the last ones

In fact, gave me hope
that I'd bag one
plus I'm a player with mine
you better ask one

Fresh out my teens
in adult situations
sampling different women
like being at wine tastings

Life is short
so a lot of your life's racing
but if you want the one
you gotta exhibit patience

this world, cold
a lot of souls are jaded
innocence we had as shorties
is now faded

R&B don't even
give me the same feeling
got my sex game on point
but, love seems less appealing

Is chivalry dead?
monogamy a fraud?
if no, then why is keeping
a happy home so hard?

Maybe adulthood
is the reason that we suffer
when we ain't fighting for love
we're stressed fighting each other

Remember letters, would you date me?
Check the box, that's yes, no or maybe?
Some changed
as grown men and ladies
But you kept the charm
to make me blush baby

you got the charm
to make me blush crazy
you kept the charm
to make me blush baby
I got the charm
to make you blush, maybe?
(you got the, woooo to make me, uh!)

You are, my light,
so real, so true
My look, on love's
refreshed, anew

I've been impressed,
but you?
I can't explain it
Maneuvered through this world
But managed to not be tainted

I'm blushing
The way I was in adolescence
And the fact that you don't try
is so impressive
you are a blessing…

Black Queen | *John The Author*

Yes,
You're a queen, nothing less
So I guess that means a nigga better come correct
Ain't none of that what's yo' name what's yo' sign shit
Tell me where yo mind at
What do you believe in?
Muhammad or Jesus
Even though they both were made by conquerors
Word to John Henrik Clarke and uh, anyway…
I'm liking your demeanor
You remind me of Queen Nzinga
Ain't nothing more attractive than Africans being Africans
And all your naturalness
Girl you got it and that's the truth
They way they tried to copy your body, girl that's the proof
I see 'em on the news, telling stories like Mother Goose
My standard of beauty is different
Girl, all I want is you
And when you walk, man I swear to GOD, you light up the world
I ain't scurred
But I am trying to build up the nerve
To say the right things to ya'
Might sing to ya'
Lord knows, I might be the right king for ya'

Ain't no endgame to my pen game
Other rappers should just call a nigga, sinsei
We not cut from the same cloth, boy I'm kente
They prayed and I came like Ayinde
Anyhow, anywho
Gimme gimme henny
And lemme see what it really do
I need a Queen of the Nile
Not a Queen in denial

All natural, fuck a weave in yo scalp
See, I'm tryna holler
as you weave through the crowd

I don't just wanna hit it,
Girl, I wanna lock you down
Cause I heard through the grapevine
Not only are you fine like great wine
You shine like daytime
Wake up in the morning and you hug yourself
Floating by like you're high, did you drug yourself?
You're charged up, let me help you unplug yourself
My Black Queen, lemme find out you love yourself…
Then, it's on girl, for real

Dance With My Daughter | *Ace Metaphor*

8 months ago
your mother told me that we would be expecting you
now, here you are
our little princess,
addressed from the Gods
God dressed you in gold
for he knows
one day, the world will come to know you as Queen Being
destined to be
greater than we
always demand to be treated as such

Look, you already have your crown
and if anyone ever asks to see it,
bat those adorable eyes of yours
snap,
then sass
say, " My Dad say it's found inside my heart"
smile,
brighten their day with that sunshine
just like you brighten mines,

and know
that I've prepared all my life
to protect those rays
to raise you right
your mother raised you right
from her belly
and placed you right
inside these arms

know,
that as long as you are inside these arms
nothing or no one will ever be able to harm you

here
your daddy's here
to guard you until that heartbeat
you hear
right now
in your ear
drumming and thumping
stops pumping
then restarts

'cause I'd go toe to toe with death just to see you grow
it feels like death Just to hear you cry
I cry too, when you do
it hurts
to even think about something, or someone
or some boy ever hurting you
or mistreating you

promise me
that the next man you will ever let hold you this close
will be one
that loves you as much as I do
that dips when you do
catches, then props you back up
spins you with his love like I do

I've been waiting all my life
to have this dance with you
your first here
right here
in the middle of this hospital to prove
that when a man truly is right for you
he will take every opportunity he has
to dance with you

no matter where
or who's looking

just like I do
and I will
but until then,
and even after when

I will be there for you every dance step of the way
from school first days
to good or bad first dates

my heart will be there to dance you through it
so place your hand right here on my chest
during the times life tries to beg you to quit
just rock right
put your little feet upon mine
anytime you don't remember the steps
then let's take two to the left
for boys will come and go
and sometimes make cry
the world and disney will try
to make you think that your happily ever after
begins with him
but I'd wipe every tear
from those eyes every time
dip you
sip you
show you
thats your happiness starts within the inside of you
you will always be enough for you
man or not
you will forever be a Queen
king or not
so let's rock and do this dance
 over
 and over again
for the rest of life
cause it's me
you
your beautiful mother…
until death do us part
and then some…

Jacuzzi | *Phenom*

We can roll in a bubble bath
Making married love in the Jacuzzi
Right after a movie
Let you control all the other half
First, Baby, let me get your mind wet

Why you wanna front?
Acting like you weren't checking me from the jump
Relaxed eye contact got you hella pumped
I'm more than just the man of the month
I'm the 808 gorilla-beating drums in your trunk
'Nomenon more than just the funk
I'm more like two skunks
banging in a crack house
Turn ya lights out
Right words from the right mouth
You wanna roll, don't you?
Let's dice out

~~Heartbeat~~
~~You make me feel so weak~~

Girl, you got me going crazy
Won't you come to my crib
And you can see where I live
Or what I'm about
Or what I done did
And maybe we could ~~(do what?)~~
Play some chess and ~~(do what?)~~
Maybe
Read a lil' bit
Get to speakin' a lil' bit
Get to tweakin' a lil' bit
Get to freakin' a lil' bit
If you like,
I'll feed you food for thought
You wanna spark the change?
I'll be there

like that song Michael sang
Won't you roll with this revolutionary-minded
Put a likkle bit of splash in your mindset
Let me get your mind wet

We can roll in a bubble bath
Making married love in the Jacuzzi
Right after a movie
Let you control all the other half
First, Baby, let me get your mind wet
let me get your mind wet

We can roll in a bubble bath
Making married love in the Jacuzzi
Right after a movie
Let you control all the other half
First, Baby, let me get your mind wet
let me get your mind wet

H.E.R. interlude | *Karega Bailey*

I walk in with the greetings
Peace Queen
She smiles and said Peace King
Me say, Oh what a sweet ting
What a beautiful greeting
A meeting of the mind
A watch is combined
To form a love that can withstand any test of time
When I rhyme
She lay the sweetest voice
And lyrics on top of mine
In love with her body
But I find
that her love gives me peace of mind
A safe haven within a war
But her love is worth fighting for
And if I wrote my love a letter
I'd write 'til I can write no more
Mí amor
I adore
Can't wait to see what the future stores for us
And I know that money can't buy love
But let's go see what's in these stores for us
Take the children on a tour with us
So they can see what love built
And perform in front of masses
So that they can see that love heals
And rebuilds the purest of life's inhumanities
Her love from back in the day has got me where I want to be
This is where I want to be,
Me plant my feet 'pon solid ground
Dem say a man is not a King
Until him find him Queen, him crown

Jack & Jill | *Dometi Pongo*

Watched her from afar at the bar
Thinking hard wondering
How should I approach her?
It's kinda odd jumping down at a club
Cause to her every man seems like a vulture
Thought about saying something cliche
Like, "Bae, what's ya' name? Tell me what you drinkin."
But I don't drink and that's really not me
So instead I took a seat and asked, "What you thinking?"
Could tell she was intellectual
Mind open as a vestibule
She turned me on without the sexual
Earth is overrated, this has got to be extra terrestrial
The conversation went from Black Panther Party
To Douglass to Malcolm
From Malcolm to Garvey
To present day problems in the Gardens and Harvey
Atrocities of armies, resources extorted from Ghana and Somalia
I questioned if I ever found the one. This was probably her
We can build from the ground,
Christ is the foundation so the only place for us to go is up
She told me I seem different
"You seem different than them other guys"
I said, "Yeah that's true"
Then she asked me the question that most women ask
"Brotha, tell me what's different 'bout you?"
See, They get high, I'm low-key
They shine, I glow
See, when I grind
It's not about material
It's about the spiritual purpose I'm really here for
So if you feel what I feel
we can go to a place where the Lord leads,

we'll never know, Zion is the road
we approach, as we grow in divine lifeline
But one day we'll be...

We still got hills to climb
But one day we'll be fine
We don't need money
What we have in God's name feels divine
And I know we'll be fine
Cause it's just you and I
But we still got hills to climb

we still got hills to climb
Baby, we'll be Jack and Jill
Lay back and chill
Jack and Jill
Lay back and chill
Baby we'll be Jack and Jill
Jack and Jill
Jack and Jill
Jack and Jill

Girls in the Hood | *Vinson Muhammad*

Young girl the world needs you to be strong and be you girl
Stay True
You ain't gotta change your hair or your style,
hit the club and be wild
Don't need to see your body, just your lovely smile
I know it ain't easy, but believe me
This is for the girls in the hood

To my young Black queens so special and precious
Growin' up on the black, Diamond, Peaches, and Precious
Mekas, Sheka's, and Nekas, and girls with African names
Jumpin' rope, hop scotch'n, playin' patty cake games
In your room doin' hair now discussin' your dream
Aspirations to sing or maybe star in movie scenes
lookin' for that fairytale like Jack finding the beans
So much hope thinking' of that life tomorrow could bring
But presently you dealing' with today,
surrounded with the world's way

Your parents tell you one thing, your streets pull the other way
It's hard to hear your heart over temptation
And all you feel you get at home is a constant dictation
The answers in there somewhere, keep the hope
And get your Laila Ali on if you find yourself up on the ropes
Hit the world with a prayer and let Allah go to work
He'll make a way, but you gotta ask first baby girl

Young girl the world needs you to be strong and be you girl
Stay True
You ain't gotta change your hair or your style,
hit the club and be wild
Don't need to see your body, just your lovely smile
I know it ain't easy, but believe me
This is for the girls in the hood

Now you grown up a little and you lookin' for love
And according to the tv, it's kisses and hugs

And according to the tv, you needin' a thug
So since you listen to the tv now you up in the club
Half naked, shakin' it, looking' for attention
Every man's eyes on you, but with the wrong intentions
'Cause they watched them same tv shows
And by those TV shows, they were taught that your value was low
They gave 'em names to call you, but those you already know
Used to check 'em when they said it, but now you just let it go
'Cause ol' boy's kinda cute, his approach like a pro
Confident thug image, just like the video
He got the same idea of love you got
Abstinence ain't on his mind
'cause it's lame to be a virgin on the block
You mind's cool wit' it, but your heart's don't know
So my advice would be to take life slow, but it ain't easy though

Young girl the world needs you to be strong and be you girl
Stay True
You ain't gotta change your hair or your style,
hit the club and be wild
Don't need to see your body, just your lovely smile
I know it ain't easy, but believe me
This is for the girls in the hood

Your world full of emotion, your mind far from calm
But for some reason you feel you can't tell daddy or mom
You ain't getting' it at home so now you're seekin' affection
Diaries full of feelin's 'bout your love connections
One reason or another situations occurred
Now you sitting' somewhere wondering' he or a her
You young and you scared, afraid and confused
"Should I deliver or abort", you don't know what to do
"Which should I choose", it ain't really a game of guessin'

Yeah the action was a mistake, but the outcome's a blessin'
Every child deserves a chance like the one that you got
So if it's a he, raise a king shinin' bright on the block
If it's a girl, raise a queen teach her wisdom and patience
Tell her you glad for her life, but how you wish you had waited
Teach her love and respect for herself and the world

Beautiful and strong, this is for the hood girls

Young girl the world needs you to be strong and be you girl
Stay True
You ain't gotta change your hair or your style,
hit the club and be wild
Don't need to see your body, just your lovely smile
I know it ain't easy, but believe me
This is for the girls in the hood

Pure | *Black Ice*

So without shame.
I exclaim
I love her.
The windhover
Between us
Remains wordless
And
Loud like Sunday choirs
We shout...
For spirit and soul
Wrapped in true love
Can only sing
Trapped in you, love
Can only bring out
our greatest we...
Give my life on loves battlefield
If she is to be
My Valkyrie.
And walk me into the next life
Stand taller than my earth height for her
in this existence
My resistance
is futile...
Ooh...
How my kundalini vibrates
At thoughts of her
And
When those thoughts occur
I'm left thinking
How thoughtful
Of the universe
To offer me
Such a beautiful vision
To feast my eyes on
Everyday
In everyway
Left full

Like ThanksGiving meals.
Our thanks given,
Spills abundantly.
Angst driven under
See,
We.
Replace fear
With faith.
Faced our reflection
In each others eyes
And
Refused to look away
From the truth
That stared in return.
We
Learn Pain is a choice.
Like love
It's a voice
That only we give permission
To speak.
We Peak
When hurts tortuous shriek
Is depleted.
Affirmations repeated
Form force field
Around our conjunction.
What gumption we have
To be so in tune
Not even the Universe
can impugn
That We perilune…
Despite gravity's limitations.
We.
Insight ethereal
Simulations so real
We can almost feel
The moon dust
Clutched between our palms.
Our story
That of parables and psalms
Of how love conquers
All.
We.
Alms for its ill-fated.

Words
Melodies and
metaphors
Memorized and restated
As if mantra
Or surahs
We.
Sight for sore eyes
That still hold
Hope in the painters
optical perimeter
The pentameter in the poet's pen
The passion upon his palate
His reason
For recitation.
We.
Resuscitation.
After being breathless.
We deathless.
Popuparly opinionated
As The contrary
To that
Which might expire.
Optimally fixated
On voluntary desire.
See,
We
choose
To be here
Refuse to see here
anything less than
Divinity.
Yet,
primitively we adore
as if we know
nothing more
than to do
just this.
Trust this will
see us through
like
new mornings

and
yesterday's lessons.
In jester ways
blessings descend
from a God
delightfully tickled
by our ascension.
Upon command
the heavens stand at attention
and
perform for us.
We
climate control.
The weather reforms for us.
For we
sunshine and warm
amidst
the cloud, cold and storm
of this living
this form of giving
is nothing short
of daily treasure.
As we create
creation
in all it's
ugly
and beauty
and pain
and pleasure.
For all those
that come within our circumference
to truly discover…
That without shame
I exclaim
I love her.
Purely.

Natural Woman | *Corey Black*

It's something about the way that you look when you look at me,
If looks could kill i would tell the jury to charge you with
Murder in the first degree
See, Im well aware of the fact that this whole look that you've got going on
was premeditated

what elevated your intentions,
was your one last quality control check before you departed your apartment
and confessed to the mirror, "I'm 'bout to kill em tonight,
knowing damn well I was gonna be in your line of sight.
Am I right?
if I'm wrong, then I won't carry on,
but it still doesn't negate the fact that you got it going on.

you are looking so fly, and I don't even know why.
Not exactly quite sure if that's
the Christian Dior, Michael Kors, or Tom Ford,
or maybe it's that sexy, nonchalant attitude that you giving off
that's translating your slightly engaged, but still kinda bored.
if u wanna be entertained, I'll make some time for it,

U so fancy, huh?
Nails done, hair done, everything did.
And u just tryin to do everything big.
Like Afros with the pick with black fist,
standing in the midst of all these chocolate sisters looking like an abyss,
at best, you still abreast with the goddesses
And even though you're modest
Every single thing about you right now is considered to be the hottest
I'm just being honest
You make a brother want to ask questions
cause I'm really trying to figure out
what's going on in, out and around your head

Sweet mother Aretha this queen's fine
this natural woman has losing track of time

In the meantime have you ever seen time stand still because I swear the hands on the clock didn't move when u walked in the room

Question:
Do have to wake up extremely early to get your hair that curly?
or do you not even trip over your hair at all?
or do you ever feel like people be hatin whenever u get it straightened?
And I think that's what got me in awe
and I just wanna watch you glow.

Whether its fried, dyed, or laid to the side
Shaved, bangs, a bun, braids or bob
twist-out, dreads, shaved heads and locks
Or even just a simple wash-and-go

All you're really worried about is keeping up with the maintenance
and maintaining its condition
conditioning it for 20 minutes with your shower cap on
But by the time that its done, its looking like the lights got cut off
and Ameren just cut the power back on
Your beauty is an extension of love coming into fruition
You're beautiful, and its kinda dope
that God is your beautician

Love, Hate | *LaRoyce Hawkins*

if love was a woman,
and hate was a man,
I wonder if they would find each other attractive

really…
if both, love and hate just walked into a bar
would they attract each other?

pay the cover charge,
notice each other from afar
and just attack each other
despite, the fact
that opposites attract each other

I wonder if it would be *like at first sight*
and love came to hate's crib by the end of the night
and together,
they drank a whole bottle of moscato

        …'cause, that's love's favorite.

so now, love's a little tipsy
soon, her dress hit's the floor
but hate says, "wait, I've never made love before."

so, love stares at hate,
deep in the eyes and replies,
"baby, without you, there is no me,
you do more than just make me,

        stop hating
          and create me.

Starburst | *Jason Williams, The Poet*

black woman,
you're the closest thing to GOD that my eyes have ever seen before.
and although I appreciate your beauty,
it is so much more the combination
of your inner strength and your innocence
that moved me to right this.

and although your emotions be up and down, like a light switch
seem like the longer that your days be
the darker that your night gets
I'm amazed everyday at the faith and courage that you fight with
Sister, you deserve an Oscar

your smile bears more healing than the palms of a million doctors
somewhere, there's a star jealous of your shine
a nickel in a piggy bank envious of your dime
a photographer whose camera has yet to capture a shot more divine
than you

and this piece is well past-due
and even more than that, it's critical
it's 'bout time that the black men in your life
let you know that you are more than your physical
and any brotha that can't see past your hips and your ass is probably pitiful

I know you're tired of the ridicule
fed up with the "hey, lil mama", "boo"s and "baby"s
joe, this mess is crazy!
out of our own mouths, we degrade you daily
and yet, you still find strength to lace your boots and raise our babies
hold the fort down while your man's away in armies and navies
Sister, you are amazing
from Harriet to Rosa Parks
the building of your structure is even more amazing than Noah's Ark

Sister, I know it's hard
but, I ain't the only one praying for you
so is GOD

So, I'mma need you to hold your head up higher than it ever was
the fact that we need black women is more evident than OJ's leather glove
I got to a point in this piece
where I felt like I'd said enough
only to realize that it was some broken souls that I still hadn't touched

so, I didn't write a love poem
instead, spit inspiration for you to hold on
your physical is weak
but, I swear your spirit, man, is so strong
Damn, we've done you so wrong
Hard to fathom how you go on
I pray to GOD this poem be the rod and staff that you can hold on

I know you're tired and your heart hurts
I came to tell you that on your worst day, you're sweeter than a Starburst
I know you're sexy in your jeans
I wanna see your scars, first

you be the star on my side, like a pair of Converse
and I know it seems
that you've been searching for your king
steady finding dudes with bling
but not an ounce of self-esteem
whole 'lotta nice things
but, don't know how to treat a queen
so, you done given up on brothas and all the challenges we bring

but, I've seen
real men change when sistas stay by their side
we have a whole different look
like a car's took to *Pimp My Ride*
hardcore on our surface
but, we're so broken inside

to all the black women in the world,
we need you to survive.

Black Love | Tebe Zalango

They say hurt people hurt people
Yah could break the cycle
Love is like a battle
and you fightin' for survival
I'm flirtin' with your purpose, Boo
I see the high you
You got too many haters ridin' by you
Them gators in your bayou is cold blooded
Just out to rock your boat
Searching for the surface, no substance
That's old luggage
You're so bold and I love it
When others sold their soul
You wasn't budgin'
No budget could take you low
Ridin' round with those power plants
Smokin' like a power plant
Alkaline water
Dr. Sebi products startup your day
Meditate to the east when you pray
Yoga mat on the beach by the waves
Namaste
I see you
You remind me of the king I need to be to keep you
You inspire the higher me
Hire me to be through
I'm on charge how we pay attention
We spendin' hours in the next dimension
I love you
Black Woman.

Love Language | *Yaw*

Love.
how blood quickens at the mention of a name
how breathing becomes a matter for wars
how bodies just know the song
how 'you' becomes we and we become a poem
i'll write it

Language.
how words shape the mouth
how certain tongues demand a particular curl of the lips and a specific opening to perform the ritual
how english is better when pidgeoned
how some of the best music i've heard
is sung in a language foreign to my understanding
i'll take the class

Love is a decision
Language a gift
cusps and wings
pain and rings
type stuff
all in
type trust

and I jump because
there is no other way

Beautiful | *Truth B. Told*

She confused me
Had me
Looking like you would
if St. Peter said your name wasn't on the list after you perished
I kept staring
She said, "Nobody ever called me that before."
And it confused me explaining to a tree that she's a tree
Until I understood all seeds need watering
Daughters should hear this more often from their fathers
All I said was, "Baby, you're beautiful…"
Ladies, you don't do "usual".
You do "Amazing"
Ain't no changing God's aim
Baby, you're a bullseye
And that bull guys are talking needs to be ignored
You are more than magazine portrayals and hip hop fallacies
Forget a five-star chick, baby girl you're a galaxy
Their thoughts about what your worth is, is worthless
You're that Proverbs 31 type chick
Read the fine print
It says your purpose is on purpose, yet a disservice you've been served
Self-esteem assassinated
Placed in coffins as we dance alongside it in a New Orleans-like rhythm
They don't get it
The magic in your movements
The brilliance in your simplicity
You make divinity seem routine
I mean…
Go ahead and rock your bonnet and pajamas, baby
Makeup don't make you
Contrary to what Maybelline may believe
Victoria's biggest secret was making you think
you needed her in the first place

Magazines don't get the picture
So stop looking at theirs to find your description
Because what this world may consider usual
In my eyes, will always be considered beautiful

Black Woman | *MelRob*

Before the beginning
of the beginning
Father Time and Mother Earth birthed the idea
of birthing a particular earthling
The elegance of this specimen was heaven sent
and it seemed senseless to fight the feeling of being defenseless
Once you laid eyes on the prize
created by Mother Earth and Father Time

The combined design of flesh with the divine
Erupted into a breathtaking structure,
appropriately named
the Black woman
Her presence gave evidence of the four elements
Earth, being her mother
The spirit of the black woman was covered by a carmel, colored clay
Crafted and shaped as an earthly display of radiance
and the cadence of her feet stepping slowly
and oh so gracefully through the universe
brought joyful smiles to the faces of her parents
Even the angels themselves were even in reverence
Of this perfectly proportioned piece of putty

She was forged in the fire and that's what made her GODly
and oddly enough the heat didn't damage her skin
it's actually what gave her that gorgeous tint
originally a beautifully baked bronze
but possessing a prism in her chemical makeup
that would allow for
other shades of beauty
to come forth out of future generations

The cooling off process ordered the manifestations of her curves
and blurbs of words

could not adequately emphasize
how water wrapped around her thighs,

and hips,
and lips,
and breast
Her chest,
the best,
her waist and face
were graced with grace
and I suppose, her nose,
her fingers and toes
though small in size,
their value grows
her clutch, her touch,
they mean so much
Because whatever she holds
turns to gold.

Earth, fire, and water
Created, baked, and molded perfection
Air, was naturally the last selection
As the wind would begin to caress
Every hill and valley of her figure
Drying off this perfect picture
Pure perfume was the aroma of this sister
And as oxygen kissed her
The galaxies came alive
The sun evolved from the twinkling in her eyes
The solar system was her rhythm
Dancing around planets of granite
Until daylight, itself would vanish
And even in the darkness, her beauty would glow
Life would come forth from every seed she would sow
Divinely responsible for populating Earth
She retreated from outer space and began to give birth
to more
black women

reproducing angelic gifts made for black men
and for millions and billions of years
she has been our present
heaven sent,

magnificent,
black woman...
often imitated, but never duplicated
black woman...

And these words are just to let you know you are appreciated
Black woman...

Not only fine, but also educated
Black woman...

Through the roughest times
We wouldn't have made it without
The Black woman...

Black woman, thank you for being you.

Mere n'a Jamais eu des ailes | *Pages Matam*

Ma Mere n'a Jamais eu des ailes
My momma never had wings
But she could tap dance on hurricanes
And played poker with death
She couldn't teach me how to be a good man
But taught me how to be a good human being
How to sit up right, stand up straight, walk tall face forward
Be proud of who you are, aint much God left in this world
But treat the world like there's still plenty God left in you

My momma never had wings
But she always fought to soar in any atmosphere
You would think that she was Shiva
The way that she juggled

      Six kids
Two jobs,   a home,
    The glory of her crown

And the abusive scars of an ex-husband
without ever skipping a beat
But you know strong women, have a supernatural way of doing these things
She said the secret to her strength
Was giving her jigsaw puzzle of a heart to God,
The only Being that has ever taken the time
to appreciate all of its pieces.
Ma Mere n'a Jamais eu des ailes

But she's always had this global warming smile
Told me to love only a woman
who could melt the polar ice caps of your past
She sat me down one day and exclaimed
"you better treat a woman as you would treat me, because if you don't
I will be on the next plane to slap you back into this country,
You are a Cameroonian man, we do not do that shit"

My mother
just said
"Shit."

But then she continued,
beware of the tempting ballad of Jazzy Belles
With tuba lips, trombone legs and a bass line
That could turn any man into a crooked song
So make sure to never sleep with no one else's bones
but your own.
My momma never had wings
She believed if you try too hard to reach for the sun
You will end up in flames. Do not be a handsome shadow of Icarus…sun
Learn how to stay grounded…sun
Teach trees about their roots, and never give the world your tears
Only smiles gift-wrapped in forgiveness
Cuz Mama said, a "Hater"…is just a person with their "Heart" all jumbled up.

Their self worth drowning in a sea of simulation
turning the oceans in their chests, into puddles of insecurities.
Because those who show you no love,

are usually the ones who need to see it the most
Ma Mere n'a Jamais eu des ailes
My momma never had wings

But damn she could fly
Could care less bout gravity
When she could bend space and time between her fingertips
She wears the fabric of the universe like a second skin.
Her first, being her will to always survive.

Understanding | *Rewind*

iDidn't Understand,
Naw...iCouldn't Understand
How You Could Love Black Men, Emphasis On Men
And Be More Loyal Than A Friend...
But What iFailed To Realize
Is You Were Me,
Me, Again...iJust Couldn't Comprehend
See...
iThink God's Greatest Creation Is The Black Woman
Naw, for real, Think About It,
He Snapped On 'Em
Her Melanin, Can't Be Described As Heaven Sent...
It Is Heaven...
Every Specimen, Is An ACTUAL Piece Of Heaven
The Sky Had Fallen And Evolved In, To The Most Special
Intellectual, Beautiful, From Head, Big Nose, To Full Lips,
Your Kiss, No Your Voice,
It Calmed Us During 9 Months Of Darkness
Your Bosom, It Fed Us, And Doubled As A Bed But,
Butt, That Rotund Brown Mound..
See How, Your Behind, Gets Me Beside, The Point...
On The Other Sides The Point....
You Birth Kings,
iMean Only A Spartan Woman Births Warriors But You Birth Kings,
Royalty, & Warriors, And Doctors And Historians,
And The Architects, Of All Of This, You Created The Creators,
That Must Make You..
God...
God Snapped On Black Women,
Because SHE Made Them In HER Image
Which Makes Sense, Why Adam Came First After You Gave Birth...
Then Along Came Her...
To Appreciate, What She Had Made..
See, iLove Black Women, iLove Black Women
So Much That iHate To See You Disrespected,
iPray For Your Upliftment
iWant To Give Each And Every One Of You Strength

When iSee You Paired With Success
iWant To Praise You, iWant To Marry You, iWant To Raise You....
iWant To Give You The World Because It Belongs To You, You Made It...
And That's Why When iWas Faced With...
You In A Rare Form, iCouldn't Take It...
You Think God's Greatest Creation Is The Black Man...
iCan Tell By The Way You Hold Our Hand,
The Way You Stand...Up For Us
When We Stood On Top Ya'll, The Way You Defend, Deflect All,
If There Are Foul Remarks
It Comes From Ya'll,
Because You Believe In The Black King, So Much
That It Hurts You From Within, To See One At Half Potential,
To You, That's So Simple...You Dedicate Your Life To His Support
You Forgive Him With No Remorse, Your Eyes Light Up When He Talks
You're Awaken By His Intellect, Because Of Introspect...
And That's What iHad A Problem With...

iTook Your Love For Mistrust
iTook Your Support For Lack Of Loyalty
But, What iFailed To See Is...
It Was An Energy Bigger Than Me
It Was For The Black King...
And A Feeble Ego Crumbles To Spiritual Things...
iHad No Self-Awareness,
iDidn't Understand
No, iDidn't Understand
How You Could Love Black Men, Emphasis On Men
And Find A Way To Love Me,
But You Did.

Black Women's Studies | *Brandon Alexander Williams*

Black woman will literally love you to death
That's all she knows
She can fix anything
I'm talking…
You treat me wrong but I still love you, Love
Because I'm a nurturer
I knew you before you did
I see you
I've seen you
I be lying when I say I didn't even notice that
I been noticed that
Feel that?
I been felt that
She be closest thing to GOD
Lowkey, she be GOD
Highkey, cause we already knew that, just couldn't put it into words
So we call it magic
She be the closest thing to GOD
Because life happens inside of her.

Niggas be talmbout, "Oh yeah, she just had another baby."
Like that be commonplace
Like that be ordinary
Like that don't be extraordinary
Like that don't be remarkable
A brotha's seed be cool and all, but
That seed sow in her tummy and grow to becoming
As big as you and I are right now at this moment, fully functioning.
That's a big damn deal.

Black woman love you to life
Black woman love you to your best self cause she believe in you
She love youYou don't
She love you
You can't

You don't love you
so you think she speak foreign language
when she talk about loving you
like... she speak me
and I don't understand a GOD damn word,
but that shit sound good
feel good as heaven

she be heaven
she fit in box begrudgingly
and you still won't know she don't want to be in there

but, she be there
she be she there
she be her in there
she meet you in there, cause that's where you be at

I could get used to this, she say
if it means loving black man
well, black boy, now
cause black boy gon' be man one day
if I have anything to do with it
which I do
he just don't know it yet
he will one day

she believe in him
she study him
she speak life into him
she speak "why?" into him
so he can see right into him
she speaks right into him

he break her heart
she teach him lesson
grow from heartbreak
and come back stronger

she reinvent herself,
...more magic

all while feeding the neighborhood,
...more magic

home-cooked meals,
…more magic
all while doing hair
in it's natural state
throw any girl at her
she whip butters like, "I can't believe it's not"
no matter the curl pattern

…more magic
no slight of hand
just caress of palm
gentle touch
she be delicate
not without strength
she read me my rights
when I need to treat myself better
so selfless…

it could've only been Harriet, bro
brothas be like: "If Harriet was a man…"
But, she wasn't.
If Harriet was a man, she might be Nat Turner; let's paint her
and he helped a lot, but she was a chess player
he like, "let's kill them all, wait & see."
she like, "let's go and keep the gun for safety
so we can build a legacy."
she protected the village on several different trips
if you tried to commandeer the voyage,
you were over with
boy, she was with the shits!

she be Claire Huxtable
comfortable in her own skin
and with yours
she be loyal before
she be loyal be-f (girl, I just met you!)
she be loyal **be-fore**!
she understands you, just so you can see her
she understands you, just so you can see her

she gives galaxy and asks you for a lemonade stand.
…really just the lemons,
she multiplies whatever you give her,

she's a giver
she deliver
she be liver
drunk in love
cirrhosis all over her
cause she love you to death

and she don't wanna love you that way
but, if that's the only language that you speak
then, she take classes in it
whatever you need, she'll have you with it
she grabs you with it
she hear people talking shit about black man
she ain't ha-vin it!

she be like:
"don't talk shit about my sun!
I rotate around him and he keep me warm!
and give me light!
moon do too!
who grew you?
where yo' mama at?
90% of black folks love they mama; facts!
99% love they grandmamma, jack!
and if you don't,
or you can't,
or you won't…
I can't relate to you.

Atone | *Jaycee Cowan*

this one's for my sisters
who stood strong through the storm
who dealt with all the lies and infidelities
in so many different forms
you see
honestly,
I feel like all y'all might be due some form of reparation
for any brotha who abused your time
or caused you any frustration
telling lies,
but, don't expect nothing from him today
because, I'm gonna apologize.

for all the times that you prepared dinner
just so he can eat
and for all the times that he didn't come home
and you ended up crying yourself to sleep
and for every female that lost their man due to some other woman
tonight I'm apologizing for all the lies and deceit
that kept you from seeing it coming

and for every guy you let borrow your car
and he forgot to pick you up at five
and for all the ones that lost their license,
and everywhere y'all go, you got to drive

and for
every time he made you a promise
and never made the promise no good
and you kept accepting his likely stories
over and over again
like next time he would
after picking you up from his usual trips to the ground
you know, like after he went and spent all of his paycheck
on some other woman and his boys,
drinkin' in the bar
then he comes home for the weekend

and just wants to lay around
for every time he disrespected you and you didn't put him in his place
and for
everytime he put his hands on you
and you refrain from smacking him in his face
and for
every female that trusted a man enough to take him home
and sleep with him unprotected
maybe you got pregnant
and tried to call him up and let him know
but his phone's been disconnected

this is for the females
and the women
and the children
living with their single mothers

tonight, I just want to offer this apology to all of y'all,
for all of these messed up brothers

'cause, Day One:
I nurtured the pain
and she still embraced me with a smile
I wallowed in my childish mentality because my heart stayed in denial
too weak to resist the tempting offers at hand
following behind a little boy, instead of the grown man

lying, cheating,
as their hearts kept beating to the sound of the same old song
"And I will always love you!"
and I wish I could've loved you too

but I kept denying what my heart and my conscience felt
I delivered blow after blow below the belt until I worked myself into the
negative on our relationship score card
leaving you all emotionally scarred
because my merit-able moments, were overshadowed by the sadness

and I'll never understand how you endured all that madness.
So this one's for my sisters
I truly apologize

New Religion | *L.A. VanGogh*

believe in me
faith have no grip on me
in hundreds of sunrises
but, I believe in you
you're my

my new religion
ready to baptize my past or
confessionals in mass
kiss a cross
where my wounds won't close

I'll come clean for you
dip my head, I'm thinking cool
I'm breathing fine
every sunrise
you look down at me
find me in the pews
praying to a cup of caribou
you're my new religion
my new religion
my new religion
my new religion
my new religion

you've got intuition
I called a star for you
but I ain't into wishin'
my new religion
my new religion
my new religion
my new religion
my new religion
you've got intuition
I called a star for you
we'll have a vigil for a broken heart

candles cast your silhouette

but, I'm thinking quiet choirs
I came in how I am
I know this ain't no church attire

but you're my new religion
my three word bible
my wine chalice
I talk with calloused hands on a clock
can you help me let go?

slipping into tomorrow
I meditate in soprano
you love me like rings and altars
why run, when you walk like water?
dip my head, I'm thinking new

my sink don't ship the same
my faucet's fair as game
my end don't mean so good
but I'll pray just like I should
your knight in shining Suge
I'm glad it's days like you're
my own misunderstood

my new religion
my new religion
my new religion
my new religion
my new religion

you've got intuition
I called a star for you
but I ain't into wishin'.

Three Queens & Apologies | *Cyrus Speaks*

To my little black girl.
Though you've yet to be conceived,
If my daydreams could sew seeds
I'd hope they'd elope with a time machine,
One that would fertilize both your eyes & mind to see,
The black queen, that I want you to grow up and be.

Baby girl I'm sorry.
For every time I'll fail you as your first example of a black man,
For anytime that I work late instead of make it to your recital or dance,
I'm sorry If you don't get your 1st car the same time as your friends,
I'm sorry if Daddy doesn't make you feel more beautiful then boys who'll try to get in your pants.

But when they try - Skip Bayless I'll put you up on game,
See how he mistreats other black girls - he'll do you just the same.
If he's a smooth talker you be a moon walker
'cause he talks like this to girls everyday,
He says you have to prove your emotions with a physical action? That logic doesn't sound very sane.

You might be into bad boys because you'll want a challenge,
Instead challenge your intellect - and work ethic cause boys aren't something you need to manage,
If He plays nice in front of daddy but behind closed doors wants to get manish,
He'll play faithful guy in front of you but behind closed doors with your girl friends he's taking advantage.

And I'm sorry if this still happens to you.
And I'm sorry if I dont do all the things I'll promise to.

And I promise to do damage to any grown man who tries to touch you,
If my friends try to touch you,
If your uncles try to touch you,
Please tell me if someone tries to touch you,
I promise won't be too hard to talk to.

Or maybe I'll seem like I am by the way I respond to your Black mother,
I'm sorry for any time her and I don't seem loving towards each other,
I'm sorry if it seems my love hurts,
But I promise you I love her
Actually while I'm at it let me address my lover.

To My future daughter's Black mother, my Queen and one day wife,
I'll say it with my chest that I'm not your king yet but for now I'm your Knight,
Fighting off all these rookie pawns who want you in their life,
you don't have to check mates
'cause this Knight is moving two steps ahead to get you right.

But I won't always get it right so, I'm sorry.

I'm sorry if I fail as your realest example of Black love,
I'm sorry for anytime my voice will test the durability of your eardrums,
If my eyes seem to rest on another woman for too long,
And if I ever make you think of me when you hear a heartbreak song.

But if your heart breaks - Geppetto I'll put it together again,
During your cloudy days I'm quiet in your storm as I listen to you vent,
I'll be your Usher, Lil Jon, Luda your lover and friend,
When you're sick I'll pick up your tampons, favorite snacks and a good movie to rent.

Destinys Child learned from the best 'cause you've been independent,
You'd run my business better than me without ever getting winded,
And I believe in mutuality so please don't get offended,
But when God entrusted this Black man to lead our family
I think He meant it.

And I need to mention,
That I may not be the best at getting all of our problems mended.

And I'm sorry for all our future damages
But moreso, because at times I may be the one that'll damage - us.
So the dichotomy of my next statement may sound dangerous,

But I promise I'll do everything in my power to never endanger - us.

Or maybe I'll seem like I am by the way I respond to my Black mother,
I'm sorry for any time her and I didn't seem loving towards each other,
I'm sorry if it seems my love hurts,

But I promise you I love her,
Actually, what I meant to say is that I loved her.

Mother, you were my 1st example of a Black female,
Once a black wife, a little Black girl –
but a Black mother I remember in detail,
You wore so many hats but never worked in retail,
You had to trash all those junk males
but you were too old school for e-mals

I should admit what I did but, I just can't. I'm sorry,
You probably think I'll treat my Black woman the way he treated you, but I'm sorry,
You probably expect me to abuse my daughter the way he abused my sister but I'm sorry,
I won't apologize,
'cause you alone chose to play the game that old con sold – Atari .

I'm sorry that I couldn't protect you,
I was ashamed that I was too weak to set him right so I left you,
It was never my intention to seem like I'd neglect you,
And who'd of thought that after years of being a stranger it'd be easier acting like I never met you.

If I could go back in time I'd say I ain't Eva scared - Bone Crusher,
Knock him out while he's – stoned, cold stunner,
I would've, I would've… I don't know what I would've done.

But I know what I can do.
I'm sorry that you were mistreated by men –
so my future wife - I'll love her,
Your son's light left you - so I'll shine that love on my future daughter,
I'll cultivate both my wife and girl into being great Black mothers,
You didn't choose good men because you weren't raised by a good man -
but your son will be a great father.

So to my 1st black Queen - no more apologies since you're now deceased,
But, if my daydreams could sow seeds
I'd hope they'd elope with a time machine,
One that would fertilize both your mind & eyes to see,
The Black king that you always wanted…
is who your son is growing up to be.

Ms. Natural | *Brown Audio*

(Sean Ace)
When I first met her
She h ad it together
She's a '69 impala
with the butter soft leather
Perm kit, couture fits
Shoe game was better
To get pretty, spent a pretty penny of that cheddar
Only thing,
Magazines got black queens distorted
Flipping more pages
and feeling less gorgeous
And she knows she's bad
But society's to blame
Compliments help
But most originate from lames
Speaking of squares
No cubicle
Pursuit of happiness for a job more suitable
At the crib, Meechy and Ms. Vaughn keep her beautiful
Miss Jessie is the new creamy crack on her cuticles
And the beauty is first
Style's after
And she get this Original Moxie to back her
She said we came too far to be going backwards
But she ain't stressed
So she don't need a relaxer

Ms. Natural, (We're all lookin' at you)
Ms. Natural, (We're all lookin' at you)
Ms. Natural, (We're all lookin' at you)
Everything about you is real,
it comes casual

Ms. Natural, (We're all lookin' at you)
Ms. Natural, (We're all lookin' at you)
Ms. Natural, (We're all lookin' at you)
Everything about you is real,
it comes casual

(Cya)
Bronze amazon
Black leather like "The Fonz"
Smooth as butter pecan
And the hair's honey blonde
And the follicle is natural
Make em all envy
Jane Carter'll give you a key to the city
Then this Carter'll give you a key cause you're pretty by design
Check the apple and the afro from behind
Rock it out of respect
young Angela Davis
And Frankie Beverly & Maze on the playlist
VH1, Soul sister
Go-getter, no gold digger
Hips ain't the only thing grown thicker
You make a cowboy pull trigger
Aim at a picture of your ex taped to a bottle of liquor
It's like that, Nubian
Your hair drew me in
Shea Moisture laying where the root begin
You make an afro pic happy
Embrace the nappy
and GOD made you that way
Don't ever think it's tacky!

Hibiscus | *Frankiem Nicoli*

Five finger discounts on this here love.
Here, here.
And all in favor say, fa sho.

Wireless days have been sliding from each other in diagonals,
The nights are sliced with samurai silence,
Still ringing with frequencies of quiet hearts,
as dull as the hum of lightning bugs
hovering a-beat
around this enchantment...

You are one and three-fourths cups of toddler waterfall...
just the most innocent precious,
An infinite affinity and the best parts are
that you are huggable and present now,

Oh man...
does a finely tuned guitar of butterfly
press heavy to my stomach when you gently twist in my bed,
Or when I think about a you being near
while a you is not and hibiscus tea kisses are missed...

Like classes on the morning breath of
having gotten too high beneath despondent moons.
Also hibiscus tea kisses are the shit.
Also, also... I love you a lot,
love you like a silhouette's best imitation of water.
Love you like the horizon's lunch break, like spontaneous continuity.
Like it doesn't make any kind of sense to the point where...
Well it's sort of sad really, that we even have to pay moments to anger and argument...
To unfastened flaws, and lions, or to any other trivia.
What of nomadic romance
be the most tender cages for taming electric emotion?

How good a swimmer is the deep?
What is this avalanche gorgeous you own?

Bring a chest to chest about this naked, I want you close.
Let me preach.
Look at your neighbor and tell something you adore it.
You can't get this glow from church.
This is the last chapter of spring's bible.

I want to wrap me in a blossoming flower you.
I'd buy a kaleidoscope to see more of you.
There's fire in my fire that needs to be put out.
You smile revivals, I promise.
Walk like a Phoenix, I promise.
You're a God but the remix,

I... remember one instance
when stars piggybacked a purple-sapphire sky.
The winds were... just about to clock out from their shift,
And through the thin film of ambient affection you...
you... didn't say or do a damn thing special,
But it was everything to be so close,
an honor to be so close to such a you... oh man.

Five finger discounts on this here love
because sometimes you have to snatch,
you just have to snatch and run and run, and run, and run and run
and run... here, here.

All in favor say... fa sho.

Lunar Admiration | *Brandon Douglas*

I've always enjoyed admiring the moon
Basking in its naturalness
It's astronomical glow
It's sheer mystery

The moon itself is a reminder of you
Helping me keep track of time within myself
Guiding me around
in this dark room called life
I admire you

Nocturnal beauty
Symbol of many things
An abundance of bad connotations
have been placed on the time frame
In which you are due to shine

Death,
broken spirits,
battered bodies
Shattered dreams
silent screams
are known to have been created
Between dusk and dawn
But it doesn't matter
if it is set
or preparing to rise
You are one of the few forces
That are able to lock eyes with the sun
That's why you have been chosen to inherit part of its energy
Giving you the ability to shine in the darkest of hours
Transforming a sky filled with dim hopes
Twinkling for dear life
into a midnight masterpiece

The end result is you
Surrounded by the many constellations

That define humanity
Along with all of the complexities that exist

Your ability to find sunshine
no matter what
Is the thing that draws me in

That solar radiance
Subtly erupting
from your lunar throne
Keeps me in awe

In your eyes
A miracle is what I saw
And your stare
Stops me so cold
I'm unable to fall

I can't move
So I just stare back

Bearing witness to the life of a moon
From first quarter, to last
From new, to full

Are they catching the shooting starts as they pass?

No, I'm not bragging
But who else could say that they've kissed the moon and lived to tell the story?

The weightlessness I feel with you is unparalleled.

I wouldn't dare compare her
to any high spell or hypnosis.

Nothing can feel like this
Nothing can feel like us

And I don't need to prove to myself

that this is reality
The gravitational pull between us
Is strong enough to speak for itself.
I will always enjoy admiring the moon
Basking in its naturalness
It's astronomical glow
It's sheer mystery
And most of all

Because it reminds me of you.

Untitled-14 | *Kwabena Foli*

what if God is not two dudes and a ghost
but a bunch of blk children playing double-dutch
but instead of jump rope
they be double-dutching with time
eternity stretched out like a long coil of wire
on one end
a little blk girl named Anais grips creation in one hand
and blk heaven in the other - the kind of heaven so cool
other heavens be appropriating it.

she gets the party started.

starts with creation
followed by blk heaven
and she be looping dat shit making all kinds of beats
this is why you can hear music in everything
if you listen a certain kind of way
by the way, Anais means
full of grace
better embrace that the birth of anything is divine favor.
Anais sends the first wave of magic
met by another blk girl named Rachel

she keeps the party going

has time wrapped around both of her forearms
lightly pinches two points of it
and she be looping dat shit producing all kinds of beats
that **just blazes** through every metro boomin'
so ageless it feels **Pharrell**.
and all the blk girls be happy
remixing the beginning and the end
till the present feels like blk magic too
and it is
cuz a third blk girl with the eye of the tiger
sees the loophole
the break in the beat

and begins to synchronize her body with the rhythm

she moves like the spirit
                she is grace in motion
                              she goes by **no name**
all praises be
to all this blk girl magic.

Sweet Love | *R.O.E.*

Dear Love,
Tell me how everything goes
I do a lot of shows and I'm always on the road
Until I get back, you know down you gotta hold
I know you think to cheat, I know you're on the go
But stay put,
'cause it's all starting to happen
I ask you "put back the bags,
Go on start unpacking"
I'll be there shortly, got kinda stuck in traffic
I sent a couple gifts
Go on and unravel the package

And you will see
I sent all the things you love
Don't worry 'bout money
Cause it didn't cost much
It may have came through music
Which came from up above
To show that better things are ahead from both of us
I'm true to you, I have never been a cheater
That's why I pen this letter to the voice of Anita
So read a little closer
Gon' step up to the speaker
I figured that I would let you know that I need ya'

She said she needs that (love)
And I promise I will give it
And I will (never go away, no, no, no, no, no)
She said she needs that (love)
And I promise I will give it
And I will (never go away, no, no, no, no, no)

Ever since we started
I saw the day coming
You gotta stay
so I don't renig on my promise
I know we clicked quick

We got a lot in common
I only think of you
In case you were wondering

I know you saw them digits
I promise I didn't hit it
Niggas said that I lost it
To prove it, I had to get it

And it was all for fun
Wouldn't do nothing with it
Don't ball up the letter
Please read it to the finish

It's been a few years,
I know you've shed a few tears
That sadness you got
I turned it into cheers

I know I can lie
I'm full of excuses
But that's all in the past
And it's all useless

So, we move forward
As the doctor ordered
We're tearing down the bridge
as we're crossing that water
so I'll stay put
good times, I want more of
So I've signed this letter
Cordially,
    Your Love

She said she needs that (love)
And I promise I'll give it
And I will (never go away, no, no, no, no, no)

For Trinity | *Tyson Langhorn*

See everybody in this music
either snappin' or they trappin'
but I'm rappin' bout the shit in my life that really happened
I ain't saying that they playin
But, to me, it ain't relating
All I know about is money,
playing sports
and being patient

got a baby on the way
I dropped a seed up in the soil
From the day that she is born
I gotta see that she gets spoiled

like her Daddy as a baby
by her Daddy as a baby
Daddy glad he has a baby
Happy happy
as I may be

I be nervous
And hoping that I never ever hurt you
or desert you
'cause I love you
and your mother
having birthed you

it's a virtue
indeed that I should use you as a lesson
when I'm sexin', wear protection
still, I view you as a blessing

and I'm stressing
and knowing that, for you, I am a rider
and provider for ya Mama
since I knew you was inside her

a survivor
is what I had to make her
I'll be glad to
cause your Dad do
want a tattoo
of your name
soon as she has you

I'mma grab you
and right before them doctors even hit you
I'mma kiss you
Was an issue
But I'm sure your name'll fit you

It's official,
My newest little friend is a girl
So I guess we can finish talking
once you enter this world.

Black Woman | *Tebe Zalango*

Truly beautiful from your hair follicle to cuticle.
Every root of you reaches beyond the sands of time.
You're the apple to my pupil,
the womb to our future
holding our history in your chromosomes, divine.
Your mitochondrial DNA gives light through my cells.
You give life to a cell charged from battery.
That one phone call got you making bail no blasphemy.
Our Creators masterpiece.
Disaster speaks when you don't hail the black woman.
Nature makes her the back bone of all nations.
Nurturers of greatness the first place you ever learned love.
1st place on this pedestal
I trace pedals from your door way to your tub.
Rub the ache from the soles of your feet
as the scent of incense and vanilla cinnamon
 relaxes you to release tension.
Untangling your locks and Blocks.
you are everything.
I just want to be ya therapy.
Whether we laugh or cry, I cherish the recipe
that life measured through the melody of your eyes.
The song of your soul radiates through your melanin.
No other touch is relevant.
Even my heart gets jealous
when you spend too much time in my mind.
So it pulls you close so it can hold the thought of you.
Then I send a text message to express this vibe.
No other treasure could compare to the charm
of your arms wrapped around my neck.
No drug could replace this high.
I get butterflies sometimes and can't say "hi"
froze in the Heaven of your presence, mesmerized.
I'm thankful that I'm alive to love every part of you.
Ya spirit, body, soul and mind.
No mistake in your design.

So if this takes the test of time
and gets found a thousand years from now,
there's no question to know how I, a black man,
love...the black woman.

This Day | *Adán Bean*

The story of this day was first written before time.
It was established in God's mind before the earth's foundation.
And what you're seeing now is how God's
providence doesn't always make a lot of sense
But it's got us exchanging vows.
This is a tale that will be told,
Of a man who struck gold,
Never my 'better half', in you - I have found my better whole
My princess-cut diamond fashioned from blackened coal,
I love you, yes, you - my kindred soul.

You know so often substance gets sacrificed for more glamorous features
But you are the ebony embodiment of the idea that both things can be keepers
Have you seen her? I have and believe me, that moment was golden,
My breath was stolen and cheeks still swollen from smiling.
Cats would ask, "Bruh, why do you laugh and grin so much?"
Well, it's because God promised you before I saw you and as such,
I could trust His foresight,
Lean on His vision
....that He knew what was best for my hopes, dreams and mission.

This is destiny manifesting - stepping ever so quickly,
While I was running towards my future, I noticed that you were running with me
So if you ever wonder why I brush the hair from off your eyelids,
It's because you're my rib
And when I look into your irises
I can see my kids.
Our house, holidays, the front lawn and cars,
The life that I see ain't easy, but believe me - it's ours.
It's a life of bill-paying, in-laws, and daycare,
I want us to stand in God's hand,
'cause I heard little becomes much once placed there
And if the Lord sees fit.
I'll spend the next 206
Years of my life

Professing to a different bone
each year why I'm honored to call you 'my wife'.
Flesh of my flesh, and yes, bone of my bone,
These arms that I have, Lord willing, will become your new home,
So let's embrace uncertainty and go ahead and turn the key.
We'll have a lifetime to learn how to love one another perfectly.

Because Yah evens the odds whenever love's given a chance
And I trust you enough to think out loud in front of you,
yet feel as though I can communicate with a simple glance.

So on this day, I give you my last name.
Because tomorrow, I may get on your last nerve,
But regardless of what happens, God will get the last word.
And as long as He's involved,
Then no situation is helpless,
And a future without you in it,
Is not mine...
...it's someone else's.

All I Want | *Add-2*

What if I told you I want to be your everything…
what if I told you that telling you is the easy part
but showing you is a better thing
you got me wrapped around your finger like wedding rings,
be still, my beating heart
be leaving me breathless,
the reason they say 'til death do us part
I love to be near you,
here you can be yourself,
I hear you, clearer than windex on glass
can't you see I'm trying to mirror you
if you are going in the wrong direction let me steer you,
steal you from whatever changed you and remind you that you still you

heal you, a love doctor and I ain't even got to bill you
just keeping it real, there's more fish in the sea but I reeled you in
and I know a catch when I see one
so I ain't gotta cast out the lines, ain't tryna act like a cast reading lines,
but if another man broke your heart
I'm asking what type of cast could I find…

see, any man can find a woman fine
fine wine and dine and call her a dime a milli-ion times
but I find that silly cause really to me that's a crime
cause not only are they wasting their money
but more so they're wasting your time
whats more precious than that?
Well that's easy
I say "you"
more precious than a fragile vase
or the name of role played by Gabrielle Sidbe,
anyway, I'm Andre
nice to meet you,
I'd love to treat you to dinner
for two in the form of food for thought

My pockets may not be able to hold do'
like a good gentleman
but I'll still cover the cost
I bought...
into the thought
of us being together,
Whether the weather change
if ever the weather rain then...
I'll be standing beside you holding your umbrella
holding your hand to help you cross puddles ...
and rubbing your hands when you cross trouble...

little did you know You & I
were already slow dancing in my dreams,
as Stevie Wonder sings "You & I"

I hope I'm not stepping on your toes
cause I'm nervous
it didn't look like it hurt you, you just smiled as if I did it on purpose,
in my eyes you are closest thing to perfect
on this earths surface
I spent my life trying to search it
so I can say that for certain
I'll gladly be a fool for you
all I can make is pancakes
but I'll learn to cook food for you

do whatever I have to do just to prove by time we turn old
you knew...
that there wasn't nothing in this world I wouldn't do for you
if you lose your mind
then I'mma be right by your side to help you find it
make blueprints,
plan out a whole life together,
decorate and design it
only ex's by my name
come with a dotted line and ask me sign it
Lady, those spaces in between your fingers is exactly where mine fit
All I want…is you…

Star | Yusha Assad

Regardless of the statistics
I know we can make it
We got a real chance at love
I know we should take it
And even though we both grew up
In a cycle of broken families
That don't have to be our cycle
I know we can break it

We can be the one couple that strives to stay strong
Even when the tough times are prevalent
The relevance of GOD in our life
Is imperative for the victory
Especially when there's no
Lasting marriages in our histories

Plus in America
Family is on the break down
Divorce rates are high
Infidelity on the take down
I'm dealing with my own feelings
Of doubt I got to shake off
From watching my parents split
And my father's car take off

from the driveway
Momma told em to hit the road
Or the highway
But daddy didn't hesitate
To ever swing my way
He took care of his kids
But the truth is I wanted both of my parents where I lived
I believe, I really believe
I've seen models of old love like Robert and Cee
My God parents ain't leave any seeds
But for me

Was like leaving a tree, of love
I'm branching out
From the false models that tainted me
With no fear of failure
Cause that's just something that ain't in me
Fear or failure, my only can't is "why can't it be?"
So talks of divorce I look at them angrily

But, I still admit that I was close to it
And my only excuse was that most do it
I've seen more examples
Of break ups than make ups
And lovers retaliating
Hoping to send wake up, calls

But when hearts aren't aligned
It don't matter how much you call
No hearts on the line
Just a black box
Occupying the space where the heart was
With love lost in struggle hope you find it in time

Helpless | *Malcolm-Jamal Warner*

I miss her.
Like I miss my men's and them when we'd play shirts and skins,
but then
still had to be home by dark.
Which sparked
teases and taunts of how I was just a momma's boy,
but all this momma's boy wants
is to be kept warm from the cold silence of loneliness.

And in the midst of all this
flesh
surrounding me, the only
kiss
that's hounding me
bounding me,
grounding me
into this resoundingly lonely state
which grates on my nerves
is hers.

Ass handed to me on a silver platter becomes a blur
Because the only one that really matters
is hers.

And I can't help it, even if I wanted to.
The distance separates us
    But she hates to eat alone.
    And I can't sleep at night.

I miss her
like I miss the adrenaline rush
of drinking an ice cold strawberry Crush
that's turned to slush after already having had 3 cans
and a pack of banana Now & Laters to myself!
Or like the first time she was in trouble and I offered to help
and she accepted and we rejected
the notion of it going any further, but the fervor with which we felt this

I knew I couldn't help it even I wanted to.

As the days seemingly turn into nights and nights seamlessly turn into days,
she likes to keep me at bay whenever I say something nice.
At first I think she just hasn't heard so I say it twice.
Then she gets even more defensive and I get even more pensive
wracking my brain
going insane over inane thoughts like
she loves me, she loves me not.
Sometimes she lets me touch her
Sometimes I get shot down without her even looking my way.
Some days I feel this ill energy being hurled toward me
and it's so thick, not even an ice pick could break it.
Should I fake it? Act like it doesn't exist and allow it to persist until I lose my mind?
Or my manhood?
It's wicked
 I, too, must be addicted because the pain feels damn good.

Yet she hates to eat alone
      and I can't sleep at night.

Some of them want to use you
While some of them want to be abused by you.
I'm so confused I do sun salutations to the moon
As I try to distinguish who's doing what to whom.
And as the sunrise looms an exhalation away
I sway side to side as conflicting questions come crashing.
Just the other day Professor Om asked if we still had passion
and I almost cried.
"No," I lied.
But through the phone, he heard the truth in my tears
replied, "Yeah, right,"
And we both laughed because he knows she and I will have passion for years
even after we leave this plane of existence.
So should the insistence of my love begin to wear thin?

I mean, she is so fine, with the most creamiest chocolate brown skin you could ever conceive,

which is just why she doesn't believe me when I speak of her beauty even in the most roundabout of ways

I see how she frowns about the ways these corny strays spout silly
preconceived pick up lines every single day, but
"I would love to bathe in the rays of your smile, so I, too, could be a pretty
brown child…"
Yeah I know, it sounds like a line too, but I'm a poet, mind you,
and I can't help it even if I wanted to.
So to correct this and to appear less didactic with my tactics
I go for more directness, but her fears ensconced by sarcasm, track this
and her response is more self-deprecating than before.
I can't ignore her plea to be loved by me, even though I'm crazed at how
she pushes me away.

Like Bridget Gray
She pulls me in. Then she pushes me out.
She pulls me in. Then she pushes me out.
She pulls me in and then she pushes me out
It's like she's having intercourse with my emotional psyche
and I just might be more addicted than she.
We more afflicted than we know. And I can't help, though
The Most High knows I want to.
But how?
Then the curse of sensitivity falls upon me. I know she needs a man who
has some, but not as much as she.
Afraid to make the stress worse, I second guess my every thought and deed
and then she wonders why I'm quiet.
Irreconcilable differences? I don't buy it.
Yet, I can't deny it.
The omnipotent silence of loneliness gets colder at each turn,
But every time I laugh the passion starts to burn yet another new hole of
desire.
She makes me laugh
I admire her wit
as much as her ass.
My soulmate, my intellectual mainstay.
My companion through the ways of these dark days.
Art hurts, but the pain stays
and maims even the most gifted of lovers
Who shutter at the thought that they'd too get caught by the less celebrated
elements of love
With vulnerability comes insecurity, which causes confusion
Because this no longer resembles the illusion
of the paradise that was one ours.
So now, as I salute the moon, it's the shine from the stars that reminds me

That Paradise does exist
For those who are willing to work for it
But the distance separates us.
She eats alone and I write poems til' I fall asleep at night
I can't help it, even if I wanted to…

Poet at a loss of words | *Karega Bailey*

Felicia,
I want you to know that there is no love
on this Earth
at this time
that will exceed the love I have for you
demonstrated daily.

Thank you for strengthening my ability
to love.

Somebody please help me,
I am poet at a loss for words.
I feel out of touch when writing about love
but I know I love to be touched by her.
As she caresses me,
it lets me know the Lord blesses me
in proportions more than I will ever earn.
And I pray that our love becomes a language
that our children grow to learn.
And may this love language be bound in a book
with more pages than our children could ever turn,
because our love would be never ending.

Lord, please allow our love to be a reflection of heaven transcending.
As love and life intertwine, our lives will combine
to create an example of what love is supposed to be.
And I vow to my wife and my children
that nothing in this world would ever be mo
re close to me.
No public figure identity, no fortune or fame,
no masters degrees or Ph.D
with credentials that follow our last name.
May we teach our children that love is right
but falling in love is wrong.
Because falling in love is weak,
but standing for love in Christ is strong.
May our love be a song,
and our lives do the singing in perfect harmony.

Together, our reflection will be called, his words and her melodies.
Only her fingers can play the keys
that unlock the lyrics that have been in my heart for her.
She is so precious in the sight of God,
That I was made before her,
just so he could work out the kinks.
And there are times when our spirits are orbiting so close,
that she can tell what I think.
Her heart resides inside me.
She is as unique as a tie-dye design.
Which makes her the only one of her kind.
So you can spare me with all your loose change,
because she is worth far more than a dime.
For a scale of 1-10 could not define her worth.

She is the woman that Solomon talked about in the 31st proverbs.
A wife of noble character, who among us can find.
I wish that I could take the hands off the clock,
so we can be lost in time for all of time.
I thank God for sending me such a beautiful woman
as a companion and friend.
And although we've been together for some years now,
I find myself wanting to court her all over again.
You know,
getting her number for the very first time.
Anxiously awaiting her calls,
together we have learned that we do not love because of,
but we love in spite of our flaws.
So in this imperfect world,
she loves me perfectly for mine and I love her for hers.

And I would tell you so much more about our love,
but the irony is.
She makes me a poet at a loss for words.

Can I Love You? | *Tripp Fontane*

You gone let me love you or what?
I mean seriously
I have traversed the entirety of Mount Everest just to reach you
Just to tell you,
those icy walls you think you're hiding behind
aren't high enough
I see you
I have repelled into the lowest pits of the Kali Gandaki Gorge
All to show you
that I have already found the valleys
you bury your doubts and insecurities in
They're treasures to me
And I'll do it again
And again
And however many times it takes for you to realize I'm serious
I wanna love you, patiently
Blatantly,
Precisely ,
I mean, I've already found the beauty and purpose
in everything you say you hate about yourself
I am humbled by the wisdom you hold behind every one of your scars
Tailored to clothe your body in strength and understanding
I don't know why you ever bother to cover up around me anymore

We're already too close for that
Close like you don't care if yo' scarf slip off
in the middle of the night anymore
I know because I always kiss your forehead
as the rising sun kisses our window pane
It's the quietest way either one of us know how to say...
That you're even beautiful when you sleep
And just knowing that you feel secure enough in my arms to rest yo' mind
provides me peace
You close like my pen and my pad
You let me play my saddest records on your eardrums
And you never skip a song
I let you read the darkest pages of my heart's journal

And you picked up a pen and told me you'd help the ending
Be a little bit better than the beginning
You know the context behind these poems
You muse
You masterpiece
You are more than the prototype
You are the concept for the content that defines these poems

I long for nothing more
than to translate your dreams into a reality
To be the prince you danced around the room with
when you played dress-up in your mommy's clothes
I'll learn the routine whenever you're ready to teach it
Until then, I'll be waiting
well dressed next to this dance floor called the rest of our lives
I wanna be for better or for worse for you
To become a better man for the worst versions of you
For our future
For your past
For every man that didn't see enough value in you
to appreciate you while he had you

You are no diamond in the rough
You are a black pearl
That was raised by a black pearl
That was raised by a bl…
Shit, you got this queen thing in yo' DNA
They don't make the double helix like yours no more
I was always told to stick to my roots
And you know I dig you…

But can I love you

So Long | *Sam Trump*

distance
can make the heart grow fonder
but they send our minds spinning in wonder
you wonder
if I still love you the same

but I wonder,
if it's all worth it
the pain in my stomach is such punishment
hurts
like a cramp from hunger
when you're lacking from nourishment, yeah

but you're the key ingredient
I mean, I'd be at peace
I'd be at peace
I'd be at peace
If I can feast
my eyes on you

you know I love you
it's true
you know you need me
I need you

even though
it's been
so long
we've managed to still
hold on

even though it's been
so long
so long

~~voicemail:~~
~~hey babe~~

~~it's been so much tension between us~~
~~it's crazy~~
~~umm~~
~~last night on the phone you got so angry~~
~~you know what,~~
~~I felt you~~
~~I know you're frustrated~~
~~and I'm frustrated as well~~
~~you know sometimes~~
~~words get lost in translation through the cell~~
~~but after that argument~~
~~I bought a ticket~~
~~I'm coming home~~

gotta turn off my cellphone
that's what the pilot said

turbulence on the way home
that's what the climate read

but it don't matter
I'm coming for you soon
the plane is revving up
and running towards the blue

in a couple of hours
your lonely days are through
I'll be next to you

so that means that there's
no more saying that you miss me
no more saying that you wish
that you could kiss me
no more lonely nights
absolutely no more phone fights

we both know that was due to the distance

we brought ourselves down
lost faith and found doubt
we brought ourselves down
lost faith and found doubt
we brought ourselves down
lost faith and found doubt

but, now
it's all smiles from here
cause I'm here, Baby

even though
it's been
so long
we've managed to still
hold on

even though
it's been
so long
so long

so long, so long…

Woman Can Stop the Rain | *Ques*

I hear woman can stop the rain.
Especially black woman.
Most
definitely black woman
All I know is her ability
so I know she can stop the rain.

Ive seen women. have pains.
Like cramp in stomach
Crunching
crying
I know woman can bench press any man
She pushes up or out
Carried and crowned
The moment that boy cry out
And when man cry out
She still has enough left to Queen his crown.
Shes as warm as the blackness that surrounds him
Even in her blindness
With eyes closed
Its still elevation
She storm
Like Xaviers prized possession
She strong. Her ancestor Katrina
She be rain cuz she does.
Reign.
Over everything and obstacle
Shes a force to be reckoned with even in her weakness.
I know
What having a back bone means
Thanks to my momma
So I know
woman can stop the rain.
Especially black woman.

Most definitely black woman
All I know is her ability so I know she can stop the rain.

I see woman in hoods
No religion
Neighbor to no man
But she knows them
Woman to be... so we call her baby
She cries in the slums
Surrounded by hoodlums
And still be the most sacred
Sanctified
We contradict ourselves by hailing her
Then turn around and give her hell

Sometimes she super hero
Native to pain
She rain dances in arguments.
But nothing changes
Drums of droughts
But it doesn't stop her twerk.
In the midst of her hurt she keeps her tempo.
Man cry and she wipes it.
She cries most nights and
Still never drowns in it

Shes the finished touch
She knows the genetic make up
Of man
From street.
Concrete
heart
Hes hard.
Made to beef with forked tongue
Gold nooses and brass Knuckles
Irises Diamond studded.
She see value.
But he be so destructive.
With himself and her
Like a ticking time bomb
Terrorist
Who only makes vows of love

In death
Who thinks showing no love makes him man.
And the guarantee of whats between her legs most definitely makes him man.
But little boy im sorry...
You first have to grow up.

Cuz woman can stop the rain.
Especially black woman.
Most definitely black woman
All I know is her ability so I know she can stop the rain.

She Sativa.
Im indicating
Shes indica
And thats one hell of a high
But They too high to see her
Glory...even when anger blow smoke.
Choke.
The damage done.
But she holds on.
Like brother forgot what a hug is
Sincerely.
He only knows what a hug was
Like momma used to swallow boy turned man...in love of her arms
Casting out all rain storms
Until he left home, now he cold.
Forgetting that woman can stop the rain and thunder
And hurt and hate
And scabs and scars
If we...allow her to love Hard.
She be God ,even with her the bullets can stop
And Just like outside closets we hang our skeletons on.
Its that concrete...That
Woman can stop the rain
Especially black woman
Most
Definitely black woman!

Future Wife | *Moementum*

See,
I am a man, see
and those that can't understand me
can't stand me
they wanna make you a family
I'm just trying to make you family
they'd rather up and leave you
they suffocate you
I breathe you
they cut you
I bleed you
they throw you away,
I retrieve you
I get my Randy Moss on,
go wide receive you
they want you
I need you

and when you need to
have somebody come to your rescue
they slow to get there
I speed through
they hold you back
I hold you down
they stab you in your back
I turn you back around
they turn you down
I turn you back up, Sista
cause I love your sound
see, I listen to you
they just hear you
I got faith in you
they fear you
they tell you your dreams are too far-fetched
I go fetch them same dreams and bring them near you
for a clear view
I'm here to cheer you

up close and personal when I meet you
they "psst! psst!" when they see you
I'm "hey, how you doin'?"
grown man when I greet you
I'm here to sweep you
up off them beautiful feet
that's beneath you
see, then dudes that did you wrong, they're beneath you
they follow you just to tweet you
I follow you, then I lead you
them dudes ain't nothin' to wake up to
I give you something to go to sleep to
play that song you wont need a beat to
they'd just rather play *Trey Songz* and try to freak you
and destroy that organ that your ribs protect
I just wanna Adam's rib you
you do wrong by them dudes,
they forget you,
I forgive you
see, they're dying to get a chance with you,
I'm just trying to live to
get up my courage and give you my heart,
like The Wiz do
they play in your yard,
like lil' kids do
they swung by,
I slid through,
I'm just trying to invite you to a party at my house
not trying to *play* or *kid* you

but I was taught to play my cards right
so what I'mma do?
I'mma give you all my trumps,
so them tramps could never outbid you,
I just want you to remember what I did do
to get you through all yo' past pain
and the best gift I could ever give you, Sista
is my last name.

For My Sistahs | *Just Flo*

Ya so beautiful
and so precious
delicate flower,
I'm here to make you stress less
Heavenly flesh, yes
you are my Earth
the Lover of all things
the giver of all birth
and baby girl,
you might not know you're a Queen
but I gotta give you props
cuz your love is all that I need
and I apologize
for any brothas that hate
they don't realize the strength and the patience it takes
to make a man out of a child
see, a lot of us – wild
but I get tamed simply just by watching your style
femininity fresh
got me feelin' the best
think I finally understand the true meaning of blessed
and it's in you
flattery's all true
props all due
to my ladies who stand tall in adversity
shine thru
watchin' what y'all do
is like bliss
so I'm en drenched with endless love
to grant any wish,
…for My Sistahs!

I Prayed for You | *Orville The Poet*

I prayed for you
I prayed for you more than I prayed for myself
I prayed for you morning noon and night
and in even in my sleep
I whispered to GOD about you in my dreams
and GOD, you know what I want
but more importantly you know what I need
I'm asking you to blend them together
and send me your heavenly recipe
AMEN
and it's crazy because,
I would give up the possibility of fulfilling my dreams
just to spend the rest of my reality with you.
and I know it sounds crazy,
but, a piece of my anatomy is mad at me.
when you're not there, it feels like my arm is missing
and when you're gone, I'm always anxiously awaiting your return
just sitting and reminiscing
and black women have such passionate lips,
that even when we aren't, it still feels like we are kissing
and fellas, have you ever wanted something so bad.
you felt like you could taste it?
Well, I imagine her lips taste like sun-drenched, strawberry intelligence.
Or better yet, gifted, gorgeous grape.
and I need see her face early in the morning, along with breakfast
and I pray you like to cook because, I'm greedy
and I always finish my plate
and she's the apple of my eye
It's unanimous
all the doctors say fruits are good for us
so, let's be fruitful and multiply
and whenever she comes around,

my body goes through some sort of strange chemical reaction
and I don't know what that fragrance you're wearing is,
but, it smells like sexual harassment.
got my eyes divided in fractions, without the long division
God in his infinite wisdom
placed you in my presence
so, it's only right, every morning I wake up we go to him with reverence
see, my past is irrelevant
our future is infinite
and we will revel in it
because, I prayed for you;
more than I prayed for myself
I just hope that, one day,
I won't have to pray about that anymore.

My Sentiments | *Lee England Jr.*

How could, I but have thought of love as only a yet fleeting moment and not a destination to be traveled?

Though my heart, an ever-so passionate melody, longing for the companionship of your delicate harmony

As a prayer, is only symbolized by the joining of two hands firmly pressed together in pure belief

You and I kissed, together in a bastardly dance created by missing father figures

A void only to be filled by the joy of your touch
warmed by
as only faith can fuel fires forged in the mind hope contains

Eyes can only now but be seen through the lens your smile becomes when you look at me

Flat-footed I stand, aiming, shooting wildly at the sky,
hoping it will fall

Bringing me closer to the star I wished upon, a time once gone, now returned

Only to feel the sweat from God's brow, watered my soul as he works diligently to help me grow
In the absence of you, my sunshine

Never more clearly convinced to, at once, shoot myself with cupids bow
As to splatter my blood on the art canvas of life for you to catch wind of the vividness my hearts words may never express

Wanting nothing more than to liken my hopeless romance to the stone that makes you stumble, trip and fall in love

Catching yourself in the rescue of my desperation to never let you go
Only then the lost may be but found

If you were to soul search the heavenly song being played by the church bells that ring for our genesis revelation

Pardon me, to not let air escape my lips as I struggle to inhale without the presence of you, divine wind

No more would I tear open a rose to find how its beauty unfolds,
than question why your response is not clearly written upon the pages of our untold story

Lest you desire that your penmanship be but a mystery
for me to solve
With only your kiss to clue my first step

I wander the path
beaten by my heart
Blindly desiring peace in the rest of your life
If you were just to but return to me
That I may know you
As we sip tea, in the Garden of Eden,
naked,
For I am not ashamed to bare my feelings for you.

How could I think of love
As just a moment
And not the way I'm going
I'm going to love, to love, to love

My heart's a passionate melody
and with you on it
I hear the sweetest song
A song about love, bout love, bout love…

A Laughing Matter | *Droopy, The Broke Baller*

You laugh like a grandmother
Rich, heavy, often . . . no . .
You laugh like a baby blanket
Warm, full, familiar . . . no . .
You laugh like a grandmother crocheting a baby blanket
A Benjamin Buttons laugh
Old as forever
Young as tomorrow
Innocent as a newborn and true to form
You laugh like…candy
Molasses trapped in your respiratory passages
Sweetening every breath you draw
And you draw four like the wild card you are
And long ago, life must have lent you one of them cacophonous coughs
that doubles as
chuckles
And all that regurgitated joy must have dripped onto your lips
Leaked into your cheeks
And petrified in your eyes
Because now
You reek of sweet
You funk of spunk
Devil's food be your deodorant
Lemon icing what you lotion with
Marmalade for make-up
Girl, fix your face
You cry Kool-Aid
Kiss cinnamon
Giggle gumdrops
And belch bonbons
Even when you don't laugh, you "snickers"
Which, really, satisfies me
And every time I look into your ice cream

I mean, eyes,
I scream silently for what every kid in a candy store clamors for
when they can't afford the whole candy bar:
A free sample, of course.
I long to lasso you with licorice and corral your citrus liquidness
Until even an Obamanomic stimulus couldn't get with this fiscal cliff
But you be laughing
Laughing like…a grandmother
The grandmother of all laughs
In fact, laughs the world over envy yours for its husky authenticity
Its unsophisticated grace seduces the muses
Inviting the unending investigation of that eternal question:
"What's so funny?"
But what's so funny
is that your laugh be more funny than what's so funny
I mean, your laugh is sick
You know, you laugh like Snoopy
Gargling Listerine
Laced with Hennessey
Raging with minty-fresh intoxicating contagion
And dogggonit, I want to laugh like that
So kiss me
Kiss me as I'm crouched at home plate with mitt open like opportunity
Ready to catch your cold
Achoo!
Bless me
Contaminate me with the nicotinged embers of your carcinogender
Until I'm driving under the influence of your influenza
Inject your violent divineness into my salivating sinuses until I cry from this
My "nighttime, sniffling, sneezing, coughing, aching, stuffy head fever so I can't rest
Medicine"
Convert my felonious fantasies into a masterpiece of melodious maladies
You goddess, invade
With your bubonic plague
Baptize me in a shower of your love in the time of cholera
Make me sick
Polio! Oh, Polio! Wherefore art thou, Polio?
Sweet sickness
A delicacy of disease
Old as Grandma's hands

Warm as their work
Uproot my canal
Corrupt my immune
Mami, in your grandness
Blanket me in you
You who laugh like a grandmother
Rich, heavy, often, yes
You who laugh like a baby blanket
Warm, full, familiar, yes
Your laugh is candy
Sticking to the roof of my mouth to be savored later
Your laugh is malady
Overpowering, it keeps me at home
Your laugh…is funny
And the joke
is truly
on me.

Maybe Your Body is God | *Frankiem Nicoli*

Divine all in your making
Psalms full of love
Spilling down your gospel, honey dense and,
...of defiance, still yielding to the air
Invisible as silence,
How our bodies sway by ceremony of braille
Holding hearings for courtship passion-
Fruit swinging below the vine,
Our Eden's, garden to garden
What a heaven blooming off you

Stained glass pleading to the lights
Busting out the earth
Giving cathedral to soil
This is service for church
Your voice is an angel in the choir
Your kiss, is bursting Jerusalem
Birthing Jesus,
Is surrendering religion

I stroke the ghost between your verses
Until a bible is double clutched by our breath
First Lazarus, Corinthians II
Our scriptures will be reborn after death
As the last prophets carved in wood on the ark
Your grace bronzing my soul in Hebrew, I feel you...
At the core of my spirit,
Holding me like a prayer...
My lord, my lord...

Maybe your body is God
And I am man
Twelve disciples thick in your text, amen
Hanging myself from the walls of your Sunday School
With harmony's noose
The second coming is a king's testament unspoken
My lord, my lord...

You are a blessing
Your love grows mountains through my practice
Hearts, gentle as wheat
Bending with the wind of Bethlehem,
Housing Goliath confessionals
Behind the stars of David
Your smile pick-pockets the sun
Gorgeous Judas,
Brilliant betrayal
I am lassoed to your faith
Baptized in flow

Divine all in your making
I leave from you with Psalms full of love
Spilling down my gospel, honey dense and,
...of defiance, still yielding to air
Invisible as silence-
How our bodies sway by ceremony of braille-
Holding hearings for courtship passion-
Fruits swinging below the vine,
No strange roots
These are from Edens, garden to garden
Lacing our lives in hymns of stained glass glory
What a heaven blooming from you...

Use Me Up | *El Thought*

*"I'm gon' spread the news
Girl, if it feels this good getting used
getting used…"*

I masturbate
I masturbate mentally
with the manifestation of mysticism in my mind
You was my valentine before time
Yo' infrared beam scream "before time"
Let there be light
In the beginning, was the womb
The essence of your thought process
Makes me want to leave my toothbrush
and deodorant on the dresser
In yo' room

You're my holy text
No latex or safe sex
F-F-Fuck porn!
Our magical memories of movies is in the clouds
We make love in the stars through storms raw dog
'cause that's the way GOD's born
And our son
He's the rebirth of a long coming messiah
Love made manifest in it's purest form
And in my shallow thinking
I thought I was looking for a wife
Behold!
A perfect angel because of her imperfections
Queen of all queens
Swindled her way through my life's poems
You the closest thing on this Earth to GOD
And it took me this long to recognize
Inside of you is where GOD lives
Now I understand how GOD feels
They say Allah speak through man to man
And through you he speaks

That's how I know that the GOD's real
Not a piece of mine
But you're my peace and mind
My soul and spirit
I'm so fuckin' logical
It don't make sense to me if I can't touch, see, smell it or hear it
I do more than just love you
You was before the word love
Egyptology
Khemetic energy
Maat
My eleven laws in place
My universe embrace
Even when I'm asleep next to you
I'm missing you with my eyes closed
I still see your face

The taste of your mind is so divine
M-m-me love you long time
I don't see nothing wrong with a little bit of bump and grind
As long as the most high sent me a sign
And he did
I had you wrapped up
locked up in my mental cage for ten years plus
So to me, you done did a bid
And you showed me submission is a two-way street
And I promise, Queen Love, I'm ready
I'mma stop being so selfish, stubborn and petty
and give you a little bit of what you've been asking
a commitment that's steady

So fight with me, against me or for me
Love me, hate me and adore me
I don't care what your shape is!
Whether you're a
Coke bottle,
Coke can,
Evian's,
or Smart Water's
As long as you season your mind with the maxims of truth
To help raise my smart daughters
And all of this randomness sounds random
But on your roller coaster, I'm randomly sinking
Out of your faucet, I'm drinking

I'm thinking I want to be baptized
In yo' water
Baby, you got me trippin'
It's December
I'm outside with polka dot socks and flip-flops
Singing real hip-hop
Talking about "I used to love her"
Shoot, I still do, Baby!
Baby, we're the perfect mix
We're somewhere between lead poison and mildew
Just ask and I will do
I'm the perfect thief with ski mask and gloves on just to steal you

The true definition of a master mason,
That eastern star rebirthed me
She didn't come from my rib
She came out whole when she birthed me
Turned me over in a 360 degree angle to pat me on my back to burp me
I feel like I ain't worthy

Baby, I don't be choosin' you,
You be choosin' me
Mentally abusing me
Put me in my perfect state to use me
So use me

Push | *Harold Branch*

When the world is in need,
They know who to come to.
It's the women to whom they run to;
Because everybody knows in a crunch you deliver.
And even though men criticize it, they realize it.
Now it's time for you to visualize, legitimize and epitomize it.
You're well pass the conception of your blessing,
In the last days of your third intellectual trimester
It's time to deliver.
And when your spiritual water breaks,
The earth will quake,
The mountains will shake
And the clouds will bow in reverence.
Your emotional pregnancy has been long and tedious.
You had disbelief in the form of morning sickness.
Your hands and feet swelled from lack of focus.
You grew tired from the many roles you had to play.
Your faith hormones fluctuated
So all of your mistakes were punctuated.
And because nothing was delegated, you grew overwhelmed.
But those nine months of lessons are over.
And now through the labor of labor
You must do what you never do-
Be selfish
And give birth to you,
The refined you,
The 'Goddess designed' you,
The 'more powerful than all the elements combined,
It's about damn time' you.
So push…
And with every surge of pain release what you used to be.
Push…
And with every exhale let go what has been hurting you so.
Push…

And as the sweat beads on your brow accept that the time is now
Not for you to wonder, make excuses, be fearful or surrender
But for you to push, labor, and do what you do best…
Deliver

Magic | *L.A. VanGogh*

what we have
is magic
Michigan State bred
purple, yellow fed
they said
all change isn't good change
so don't throw your heart away for pennies
magic

but i'm two cents away
magic
and who said I can't levitate?
magic
like flying
I was promised wings
a wager
promised a cushion in space
those tricks
expelli-harmless
but I heard a cloud say
someone must pay the sky
for all this galaxy in me
or land owes
magic

my grandmother told me say "thank you"
even when you didn't ask for anything
so, thank you
for loving me
all the self I left back on 25th street
thank you
for putting freedom back in my bloodstream
my blood cells marched towards hearts
protesting a love I couldn't yet understand

but you spoke
you million man speech'd all through March
and we spent April spinning vinyls

how do I fall for you in my dreams?
sleeping next to quantum physics
you make time feel so elastic
magic
isn't that your favorite player?
magic
you give me light
so much my garden grows towards you
magic
what hat did I pull you from?
Magic
I've worn so many in my life, but magic
I hope this is pure talent
not distraction
not magic
but magic
just magic.

Relax Her | *Jus Cuz*

She on her grind
So she's working all day
and still look good enough
To turn heads her way

Ask if she's alright
She'll say she's okay
But deep down inside
it's all work and no play

She got her own
But it's okay
To take her hair down
Make her queen for the day
Make a scene out in public
So she's seen in a way
As the perfect compliment
To a King
I must say
She deserves a standing ova'
And the utmost respect
Like a pupil's sinsei

She works hard for the money
Even harder on her tummy
Looking the best
When she's claiming
that she's bunny

What's funny is she don't need much
When her ground gets shaky
You can be that crutch
When she feels all alone
You can be that touch

That's not a million bucks
But it's worth just that much

When the pressures of the world
Weighing on ya only girl
It's the power of a man
To make her toes curl
Just relax-her
relax-her
relax-her
relax-her

When the pressure start building
And the stress got her illin'
If she only got a hunned'
make her feel like a million
Just relax-her
relax-her
relax-her
Be her relaxer

Mother Nature | *Limitless Soundz*

Mother Nature let your roots grow
Mother Nature let your roots show

Galaxy in your eyes
hair defies gravity
the way you rock yo crown, I just bow to your majesty
Goddess Oshun,
I be the tide to yo moon
I see the light through yo womb,
you give life to the tombs
resurrect the new intellects that would fight for your wounds...
lovely long locs, perfect bride for a groom, no lie

(he ain't lying) don't try to hide your truth
that synthetic only covers up your roots
out that scalp grows the tree of knowledge
expose your fruit
passion when you speak, if it drip, then I catch the juice
on the rocks and couple shots it got me like, ooh
Can't take another shot, girl, my heart ain't bullet (proof)

be natural unapologetically
held sacred like a deity or delicacy
elegant, eloquent, sheek
embellished antique
intelligent speech, forever effortlessly

you bend light with yo smile
the sun reflects from yo shine
Life-giver
I just wanna give you life through these lines.

Savior | *Matt Simpson, The Man of Culture*

In church, they teach about the love of God. We learn concepts of being covered and being saved. We learned to sing a song like, "we've come this far by faith." And I love that because, all of it is true. But I don't think our saviors have been given enough credit. Black people have been saved over and over and over again by our mothers and sisters, our aunties and big mamas.
By you, Black woman.

Your voice. Your voice is so sweet. Your voice is like a song to me. But your voice is so strong to me. Your voice has validated every significant social movement this country has ever seen.
You Black woman.

We know what direction to go because you have shown us every time. Queen Sojourner Truth, you challenged the suffragist to see the humanity in Black people, especially Black women. Mother Ida Wells, when you saw your brothers being strung from trees - tortured and executed, you invented a movement, an anti-lynching campaign that made the nation stop and pay attention. Mother Kathleen Cleaver you taught us what Black power is, and showed us the strength and beauty of a Panther.

That's that voice. That sweet voice is a reflection of your wisdom. And that wisdom will always be our saving grace. We are saved because of you.

There's a certain poise and grace about you, your physique, your whole aesthetic. Your body is fine.

You've put your body on the line to cover us so many times, protecting us over and over and over again. You, Black woman.

Mother Harriet, you risked your life to show us the way out of bondage and into freedom. Mother Mary Bethune, you built institutions and made safe spaces for us to sharpen our minds and explore our souls in peace. I think about the plantation, and imagine how many children you accepted as your own after the auction block ripped families apart. Or how many times you

offered your body as a living sacrifice to protect your daughter or husband from master's lust and hatred. You put your life on the line to cover us. Your protection is divine.

What does it feel like to be "saved?" what does the Holy ghost feel like? It feels like love from a Black woman, like "fire shut up in my bones." It's spiritual. Godly.

If we've come this far by faith, then the truth is Faith must be a Black woman. And as a people we owe that sister everything. I'm addressing you as savior, Black woman. Thank you.

Ode to the Magic | *Pages Matam*

to say you are only just black woman
is to not understand the fullness of the earth
it is to not see how you make time want to fold unto itself just to
experience the remix of miracles every time you walk by

Your smile is an echoing miracle.

I asked the sun: *how do you know which color to glaze her temple?*
How do you make honey of your rays pulling her pores to more of your freedom?
The sun replied: "you should know it is not she but I,
am the one who tastes her skin,
so that I can remember where I come from."

How many rainbows did it take to form you?
are your bones made of joyous laughter?
did the fire in your eyes potty train the big bang at gunpoint?
or was it the wrinkles in your hands that taught phoenixes of resurrection?

I ask such questions
because I've always wanted to know what it means
to be a sky trying to swallow an ocean

to be purpose, or a reason
though this world will rather often leave you hanging
But you are no one's apostrophe,
With not a need to be saved, or to be made complete
You just want to be
With your universe
Shining like a lighthouse
And all I want
And all I can work for
Is to always be worthy
of your shore

Girl | *Pugs Atomz*

Dream bigger, be bigger like Yaya say
Oh that's the new you?
Well, enchante'
Gotta sort yourself out
Find your feng shui
I'm still trying to get it like every day
Humbleness is hard when you start receiving praise
But realize some words just can't be taken away
Gotta do what's best for you to make life okay
Peer pressure is a mutha
Might ruin your day
See, I say no go
So much to get there though
And the people will judge you by those photos
I know who you are and they just don't
Don't let 'em steal your joy
'cause they just want you in that same old predicament
Misery love company
Think on it
Pray on it
Sip a cup of tea
Never let the world be broken into borders
and I'mma tell you like I would tell my daughter

Rose Gold | *Steve N. Clair*

Your love only intensifies with age,
never crack, never fold, my Rose Gold.

I tried silver, but she never delivered,
I gave platinum a chance, but she never
truly appreciated my romance,

So now I'm revising my daily conversation
with my Creator like, Heavenly Father please,
If you can grant me with one of the finest
pieces of your jewelry,

I guarantee, that I will be the best man that you
created me to be,

Then all of a sudden, out of all of the options
within the Universe, and I mean dozens,
the Lord sent me a delicate gem, very fine
in texture and structure,

Your light is radiant, difficult to describe
like no other,

Now do not be alarmed about that, as your
glow is vintage, rare, and true,
I cherish every drop of copper inside the
melanin, that was formed inside of you,

never crack, never fold,
Your love only intensifies with age as we grow old,
My,
Rose Gold…

Melanin | *The Boy Illinois*

Yer!
Brown skin curvy and thin
Fine details
bout important as an ad lib
we gon' prevail

'cause she done been through the same struggle
she know me well
try to make us hate each other
but me see no evil

even when it don't come out clean
you know that I mean well
was playing this on YouTube
and I sent it to your email

She know I'm 100 with it
and she know I run with it
but you get the best out
when you let the sun hit it

Melanin | *T.L. Williams*

Blow some racks on you 'cause it's necessary
I get all my juices from a darker berry
You the type of Queen a King will wanna marry
They just acting extra cause they ordinary
Like hop in let's go for a spin
I mean I'm digging your skin
To real for me to pretend
You got me coming and going and coming and going again
We can be homies and lovers and friends
Make you believe in the man
I'm trying to win
Shine like the sun cause you don't need a tan
Snowflake won't hear from me ever again

I'm in love with you Melanin
In love with your Melanin
In love with you Melanin
Black power is all over your body
All over your body
All over your body
All over your body

Blow some racks on you, cause it's necessary
Thirsty, get my juices from a darker berry
Actin extra cause you extraordinary
Queen for a king, make me wanna marry
My, angel in disguise
I'm attracted to that Black girl magic I just can't deny
I'm mean I'm talking me on you on you on me
Cause all I wanna do is unify
Girl, let's unify

I'm in love with you Melanin
In love with your Melanin
In love with your Melanin
Black power is all over your body

All over your body
All over your body
All over your body

Baby the system know I want you
And the systems know that you want me too
They just don't want us to procreate
So take off that dress before it's too late

Star | Yusha Assad

Regardless of the statistics
I know we can make it
We got a real chance at love
I know we should take it
And even though we both grew up
In a cycle of broken families
That don't have to be our cycle
I know we can break it

We can be the one couple that strives to stay strong
Even when the tough times are prevalent
The relevance of GOD in our life
Is imperative for the victory
Especially when there's no
Lasting marriages in our histories

Plus in America
Family is on the break down
Divorce rates are high
Infidelity on the take down
I'm dealing with my own feelings
Of doubt I got to shake off
From watching my parents split
And my father's car take off

from the driveway
Momma told em to hit the road
Or the highway
But daddy didn't hesitate
To ever swing my way
He took care of his kids
But the truth is I wanted both of my parents where I lived
I believe, I really believe
I've seen models of old love like Robert and Cee
My God parents ain't leave any seeds
But for me
The model they left
Was like leaving a tree, of love

I'm branching out
From the false models that tainted me
With no fear of failure
Cause that's just something that ain't in me
Fear or failure, my only can't is "why can't it be?"
So talks of divorce I look at them angrily

But, I still admit that I was close to it
And my only excuse was that most do it
I've seen more examples
Of break ups than make ups
And lovers retaliating
Hoping to send wake up, calls

But when hearts aren't aligned
It don't matter how much you call
No hearts on the line
Just a black box
Occupying the space where the heart was
With love lost in struggle hope you find it in time

The Art Institute | *Que Billah*

You will walk forever, leaving footsteps in my mind.
I can see your beauty, there's nowhere that you can hide.
They don't understand you, they gon' keep telling you lies.
But, you don't owe them do not live in their eyes.

Damn girl, I see you working hard, you like a work of art.
You too fine to be working this kinda of a job
I know it takes some heart, you beautiful and smart.
Some girls play their role, but you could play the star.

Spotted you from a far, you shot across the sky.
I was on the pharcyde, you was passing me by.
And by the looks of it, you was in a zone
Tired as hell on the EL
on ya way home, from work.

It was a first seeing somebody this fine,
waiting on the blue line
smelling like French fries.
I realize there's a purpose that you were born.
You're like a Unicorn in a Mickey-d's uniform.

You will walk forever, leaving footsteps in my mind.
I can see your beauty, there's nowhere that you can hide.
They don't understand you, they gon' keep telling you lies.
You don't owe them nothing, so do not live in their eyes.

Gift | *Rashad Tha Poet*

The Black woman is gift
say her name
say her name
but never let it drift
from the tip of your tongue
let her spirit stain your heart
cause she stays unsung

we gotta reframe the narrative
hang our own pictures
depicted in the scriptures
our history was stolen
mouthpiece was golden
but now we pimp verses
or either Times Square with them purses

but we gotta realize
that her womb is the workshop
where GOD creates
and everything is perfect
he makes no mistakes
she's sun-kissed
only a fool could hate
that's why I can't understand
the absentee rate

now, she's the most loyal
yet the most betrayed
we gotta honor her
though she's underpaid
and undervalued
but she's much more
not just Prince
we all should adore!

signs of the times?
yeah we on our grind

but we can't forget the Queens
the reason why we shine

now, we gon' work it out,
we gon get it back together

Letters to Sister Betty | *Daunte Henderson*

Walk closer to me.
I'm not waiting for you. Just
preparing for you.

Dreamers | *Dion Jetson*

Be who you want
You were born with that right
Birthed the whole world
And you still gotta fight
They say you ain't equal
Like you ain't give them life
Like you ain't give them days
So many sleepless nights
No time to dream
No dream to follow
ONLY a wife and mother
Those dreams too hollow
This ain't no diss
I promise you that
You can be anything
Plus that
Be a doctor or lawyer
You can act you can rap
Write your own story
Bridge your own gaps
Don't listen to these people
Who say you good only for laying on your back
It's not your job to make up for what they lack
Born a woman, but you to can be a dreamer
House on the water, every year a new Beamer
Without dreams, Whitney would never be a singer
With dreams to pass down to Bobbi Kristina
To all the little girls with their hair brush singing in the mirror
For the sake of us, I need you to stay a dreamer

Sistuh Girl | *Keith "Keboi" Rodgers*

When Eye first saw you, Ahhh you were the truth..
With that slight gap in your tooth..
And them dimples in your jaw, Boo...
And you drove me wild with that pretty smile
and Child...
you had your own little style..
Fingernails painted and filed...
Oh excuse me shy Queen,
I mean
manicured...
Proud and pure
and of yourself you were sure...
willing to endure
Any pain, any strain, any stain, any rain, any shame, any thang..
To be independent of any man
who tried to get his hands
in your pants..
What did he stand?
With you, not a chance..
You said romance was for the Romans
But not for this woman..
You said roses were for the noses
That like that garden smell...
But you say when your garden was hell..
Where was a man, then?
Out hanging with his friends, drinking gin,
committing sins, probably ain't been in
a committed relationship since they don't know when...
probably since they were ten.

Now they are out having fun,
thinking they're the bomb,
creating daughters and sons
but by society they are getting shunned

because they are shooting guns
at the ones that were black
from the other side of the track..
Didn't pay you any mind because you was skinny with no back..
Oh you tried to get fat
but the little food you ate,
wasn't enough for you to gain any weight..
Because you were struggling through college working late,
eating memories off an empty plate
Trying to graduate..

it got to the point where they started to say,
"you must be ain't straight!"
Because you didn't have time to let them play games with your mind.
Oh, you weren't blind...
It was a few who you thought was fine.
but they were so doggish and fake ,
they would take any girl out on a date and if she fell for the bait,
ended up in Motel 8,
in the room with the cheapest rates..

but you
you had visions and dreams of bathing in rooms with steam in the air,
on back of the chair, in your hair...
From the hot tub
because you got love for your body and soul,
that black gold,
that butter on a roll,
that sweetness in the candy jar,
that..that...well,
you know what you got
because you know what you are, a Star
with your own heaven and space...
thunder and lightning is the treble and bass that you dance to,
education is the only man you let romance you...

many nights you have cried until your eyes were dry...
because of the things you had to sacrifice to get a better life..
You thought you wouldn't make it,
you thought you couldn't take it
because the odds were against you...every since you
enrolled negativity took its toll..

but you kept your head up
instead of your legs up,
every morning made your bed up
and read up on your homework..
stayed in touch with your home church
and asked the congregation to keep you in their prayers
and they must have done it..
because a scholarship, you won it..

or should I say, you earned...
your lesson, you learned it.
you studied so intense until you burned it
with desire,
your eyes had that fire,
your heart had that passion,
your mind was about action
and you were wise enough to realize that school was not a fashion show...

sometimes you wore the same pair of jeans
2 days in a row
and if the clothes weren't on sale..
they stayed in the sto'...
and through all that...
they had the nerves to say you think you're all that!
aint that something?
but let me tell you one thing!!!
when you get home tonight...
I want you to light
yourself a candle and take a much deserve break...
for your own sake!
they just trying to Playa hate...
you put on a little weight in the right place...
got a nice shape and I am honored to say...
that it is YOU who I must congratulate!
Although I have tears in my eyes and a smile on my face...
I'm not kidding...
           Congratulations Sistuh Girl,

                      You did it!

Body Positivity – *Brandon Alexander Williams*

I'm writing this letter to let you know…

I bet you don't know that,
I gawk at you in awe when you're reading
and when you throw back
the page that you just finished completing
and when you show that
You love yourself before any people
Shawty you so apt.

greatest of all time down the median
How you go at
life and every thing you believe in
and study on that
and battle depression with appeal
you know how pro's act
Uh huh
you know that Pro-fessionalism
I've always dug your disposition
I bet that you get it
from Mama, when I met her
I knew she never knew different
than royalty, and poise
with a lady's precision

I brag
about you often and
Told my Aces: "her self esteem
Be so damn awesome, it's
Bonecrusher song with TIP
Killer mike all in it
mixed with a very crooked mechanic
Neva scared, only confidence

Taking advantage
of all of this

6-foot 7 minus 5 inch
chocolate
Skin occupant
Living monument
descendant from Mama's Mama's Mama'nem continent

I like the vibes you've given me
I'm all about the body positivity
wouldn't care if you weighed about infinity
Pounds,
That's a lie. I'd be concerned about Ability
and health
agility and how you see yourself before I offer sympathy
Of course and
In the future,
Want you to always feel like you got choices
Don't want you to end up an
unhappy housewife that forced it
Hella remorseful livin

If I didn't dig your character
If that's the really case,
this statement instead would be
congratulations on the pretty face
That's what I'd really say
That's what I'd really think

You ain't gotta be a supermodel
I don't need validation of your beauty from others to choose to dawdle
in your presence and fervor
and leave sunflower as is
not pluck out of dirt & then hurt her
Even if I got a greenhouse
to nurture her, Further

Cause she don't belong to this
Ain't no ownership
but if she choose to come over and be
I'm all for that shit

She in Her | *Zeaux Indigeaux*

Black Woman I love you, because my mother loved me
Countless days in my youth I watched her slave just so she could see me free
Sacrifices unimaginable, and she would do it all again according to my older brother, clearly I am the proof
A Black Woman's love knows no glass ceiling or porcelain roof
Her two sons, well-born into compassion and truth
Marked with this melanin, worth more than gold- it's no wonder there's a market for Black men
They like us to play hangman, we like to play jumpman, not realizing it's all part of the same plan, to be a spectacle-high above the crowd to symbolize how we don't fit into society
But it was my mother who taught me irony
I am her angel, that's why that Black boy fly, see she changed my view
Given the gift of vision through these brown eyes that know love when they see it for true
Black Woman, you hold the same face of my mother and so I undoubtedly see it in you
You hold her crown as Queen and I've been told heavy is the head that is endorsed
In the same vein, my mother gave me hair of the lamb-praying her sons would embody God's will, our follicles were just following the coarse
Kinked and coiled, together they stand, strand by strand intertwined
Like space and time
That's like, having you here and having you forever
Our struggles akin and our consciousness tethered
I was taught to connect with you once my umbilical was severed
A Black Woman held me so I seek to hold on to one dear
A Black Woman's love doesn't intimidate me because it was a Black Woman who taught me not to fear
My light when I was scared of the night-helping me realize that without darkness a star won't shine
Now I seek her that is darker than zero hour or falling back sixty minutes like daylight savings time-
I, want my woman darker than indigo so that our children will be the ink that rewrites history

I'd pick her continuously
Time and time again, reaching out and letting the dye from her touch stain my soul through my hands
Same hands that used to clutch my mother's as she led me on the right path
The one I walk to this day too
My humble beginnings were the foreshadowing to me ending up with you
Intersecting on this plane just so that we can end up being parallel to
With the only time I take the forefront being when they come for you
I'll lift you up because that's what my mother did when I was knee high-desiring to see the universe in my mother's eyes so bad that mine would cry
"It's alright" she would say and I would feel as she levitated me towards what I believed to be the true height of the sky
Now your consolation, you can find somewhere in the constellations, with stars strung in your name as I propel your glory to that of the most high
It's just some things I've come to recognize
Like, that you, Black Woman, are food for the soul
Reminiscent of the nourishment my mother provided on infinite mornings, noons, and evenings-from out of the oven and from over the stove
She created my favorites and better still, created an appreciation for that which I may not have a taste for
Whether savory or sweet, you're what I crave more
And a life without you is no less worthless
No fulfillment, just thirst and hunger
Like how badly I wanted to learn when I was younger
Because my mother had book after book on shelves to satiate the mind
And after she helped me associate the alphabet into words, and words into meaning, that's how I spent my time
So, I have no problem taking precious moments, just to be knowledgeable about you,
Discovering what you have to teach me even if I only learn more about myself in the process
I'd research with the utmost of effervescence nevertheless
Black Woman
How can I thank you for having my back when it was bent, bruised, and bloodied
Sequential to the preceding of my mother placing her hand on my chest so that I would sit up straight as I walked, talked, and studied
Proving that it is you who is my back, not my wish bone
I can't just break you down like it will yield something better than what you've already shown
If I'm in your heart then I'm already home
Because I felt my mother's heartbeat in the womb before I even noticed my own

That's how I know my chest won't rise nor fall rhythmically without the melody in your voice
A drumming in my ribcage, picking up the pace with a resounding rejoice
Celebrating the divinity within God's choice-to bless me with your presence
How since I've stopped being able to attend church with my mother, I've ceased to feel that same essence
Hearing hymns because it was her who found it important and remained adamant
Maybe because God is omnipotent but his auspiciousness is quite limited without a host to be the catalyst, or
Just maybe the Father needs one who has the makings of a mother to be able to reach the son as an advocate and all other mediums fail to be adequate, or
Look, I apologize if I'm rambling or if my words sound odd, but I say all that to say it was a Black Woman who brought me closer to God, so I pray, I pray to have one inshallah in all awe
Though together we may be flawed, your love sounds perfect to me-just as I know my mother's was a purity
Let us not let the general misconception of how we as Black men see you drive us both into obscurity
If there is anything in which you can take security
It is that I will forever love the diaspora of you and these words telling you so-flow with just as much anticipation that you would hear it as the inspired appreciation took my hand to write
And though they may try to model many after you, none will quite match the unequivocal archetype
The Black Woman

24 Questions: A Handwritten Letter to Peach | *Dexter*

Dearest Peach,
    I will start this letter by quoting the contemporary literature of the late great Nathaniel Hale and his good friend Curtis Jackson III…

[insert "21 Questions" intro + Hook here]

I got some questions for you. I think there are more than 21, but here goes…
1. Have you ever been in love?
2. When did you first experience heartbreak?
3. Have you ever fell out of love with someone or something?
4. I believe one has to know one's self to love one's self. Do you know who you are without a doubt?
5. Do you love yourself?
6. How much?
7. How do you know?
8. When did you discover self love and choose to choose your well-being over others'?
9. Have you ever loved someone? If so, how did you communicate that?
10. Do you think it was effective?
11. What are 5 ways to say "I love you"?
12. Can you love someone and still make mistakes that can hurt their feelings?
13. If you love someone, is it forever?
14. What makes you feel loved?
15. How do you know that you are loved?
16. What do you do when you aren't feeling loved?
17. How do you feel when you aren't feeling loved?
18. What do you absolutely LOVE (not like) to do?
19. Are their different types of love? If so, name 3 to 5 types and how you'd define them.
20. What exercises do you do to make sure that your "love muscle" is always on point and operating at its peak?

21. Growing up, which parent did you crave love from the most?
22. In what ways did you desire that parent to display or show love to you?
23. What do you think your strength is when it comes to love?
24. What do you wish to improve or strengthen when is comes to love?

Peace, Love & Light,
Dexter

P.S. Can't wait to see you Friday (Lol) :-)

Adam's Rib | *Chris Wiley*

You were made from Adam's Rib
My love is surrounded
By your presence

They say home is where the heart is.
You are not my partner
You are my equal
Most people
Don't understand
You are the lung that allows
Me to breathe.

Inhale
at a different depth
And magnitude.
Sometimes I forget to
Hold the door open but I promise
Baby girl, I'm not that dude.

You are the spirit of the mind
Like 20 year old merlot
I do get better with time
I want to sip while I worship
slowly
Infatuated by your holy
Caught up by your grace
I'm determined to be the only.

Drone.
No sight
Controlled by your admiration
Faith flown
With just two wings
It's my first time and it appears

That loving you has become
My full time occupation.

Your love is like a staph infection
Deeply incased in bone...
Density vastly approaching the age
Of Mr and Mrs with intensity
Other men are attracted?!
Competition..
Enemy.
My inner me.
Screams.... differentiate.
And show her what's meant to be.

My energy
We are them
This is we
You are us
Chasing kids
Down the aisle
Out the door
At toys R us.

The vision is clear
Sometimes the mission
I fear.
Defeat haunts me.
A sinful man that
Prays for a godly woman
That wants me.

Inseparable.
She is the crowd
I am the the stage
She is the book
I am the page
She is the loc
I am the braid
She is the cotton
I am the slave...

A goddess
A Queen
A consort
An empress.
A diamond of the world
Better yet you are priceless, like pearls

Skin rich
Thick hips
Full lips
Black is beautiful
From the natural hair
All the way down to the cuticle.
I stand back and visualize things
That I would do with you.

I embrace your silhouette
Ancient romance kind of like
Romeo and Juliet.

Character like silk
Soft, but firm
Mind of a teacher
I want to learn
A student of your devotion
Mesmerized by your beauty
Frozen
Vulnerable
Open
Because a black woman's
Curriculum
Runs deep
Like a bottomless ocean.

Black woman is knowledgeable
In control, intelligent.
Your womb is an incubator
For Princes and Princesses
That grow into kings and queens

So without you there is no throne
Without you I have no throne
Our names are on this doorstep
So without you, this is a house and not a home!

Genetics knows about you
But, they cannot clone!

You want to know how to make a woman mad?
Post a picture on the internet and then
Not answer your phone!

The beauty of a woman is far beyond
Any mans understanding.
Standing in her presence is more
Than just a glimpse of her essence.

World teaches us how to lust
Through TV and magazine
But, videos and centerfolds
Do nothing past the visual.

I want to hear her thoughts
Spiritual....
Touch her face
physical...
Watch her walk
Sensual....
it's pivotal
That every man experiences
These things,
Because A woman is more than
Just the flesh of the opposite sex
She is simply
Everything

Myth | *Kwabena Foli*

happily ever after
is
a dangling
carrot

keeping you
from
the happily ever
now.

Points | *Daunte Henderson*

Treat you like you extraordinary.
Whether you got flowers from another seed, or
you look like Halle Berry.

Treat you like the special edition.
The $18.99 Blueray with the glossy cover
or the 1+1=1 addition.

We vision. We see eye to eye.
Sky to sky. The flyest thing is
that we synch. The only thing is that we wifi
With a firewall called miles. 677 to be exact.

She's a Blessing | *Drunken Monkeee*

It ain't all about ya looks
It ain't all about ya eyes
It ain't about ya waistline
Or your broad size
She's a blessing
Oh Lord,
She's a blessing

It ain't all about ya looks
It ain't all about ya eyes
It ain't about ya waistline
Or your broad size
You're a blessing
Oh Lord,
She's a blessing

See, she's an angel GOD sent from the heavenly skies
She's the truth instead of a lie
She's the light that outshines the dark
She's the bandage to a wounded heart

She's the pearl
She's a diamond
She's worth more than gold
She's that good feeling that make the Black man
Hold on when he wants to let go

God hold the world in his hand
And when the time is right
She could hold it in her stomach
See, I'm hooked on yo' beauty
Like a conscious man is hooked on knowledge
See, you love instead of pain
She's the sunshine instead of the rain

If she was the world
She would be happy instead of insane
My love for her is deeper than the Mediterranean Sea
Whenever I hug her,

The vibe, the energy
Make me feel like a warm baby
Wrapped in a warm sheet

So excuse me if I get too deep
But, see that's just what she is to me

She's Oshun
She's beautiful
She's more than just great
Her body could be able to produce earths and lakes
She's a blessing

Don't You Know | *Chris James*

you remind me of a time
right before I realized that parts of a female anatomy
weren't necessarily nasty,
but quite the work of art
unlike the boys on the playground had convinced me to believe

told me that females had cooties
and that they came from Jupiter
which somehow made them stupider
see, they had me female-woman-hating
like Spanky, Buckwheat, and Alfalfa
but, boy was I a fool to believe those *little rascals*
come to find out,
they was trying to keep all the ladies to themselves
just selfish

it's amazing
how a woman is so masterfully made
magnificent masterpiece
handcrafted
designed divinely by the hands of GOD
kissed by the Sun
hugged by the universe
orbited by the moon
consumed with light
pregnant with possibilities and infinity in their wombs
the power of monsoons in their touch

I have never seen anything
more beautiful
than a woman

see, not even the rise of the sun in Costa Rica
gleaming against the face of the mountain

reflecting on clear blue waters
could compare
to the rare imperfection of a woman

I have never seen anything
more beautiful
you have never seen anything
more beautiful
than a woman

you have never seen anything more beautiful
than an angel
carrying life
all for the sake of life and love
held on by an umbilical cord
see, her labor is the very gateway into life
as GOD's grace is the very gateway into heaven

and for that very reason
we should cherish each and every woman
and the ground they glide on
rose petals at their feet
be constant reminders
that they are royalty
born only to be queens

women, you are more than a piece of meat
but, the full course meal
slowly prepared in Heaven's kitchen
mixed with all the right ingredients
and seasoned to perfection

see, you are GOD's art
you hang on the walls of our hearts
it's no secret
that you are GOD's greatest creation
I thought it was necessary to remind you

because, I have never seen anything
more beautiful
than a woman

B-E-A-U-T-I-F-U-L Spell | *Toni Mono*

Black beauty beyond body
bold, with a brilliant brain
Beautiful as a butterfly, flyer than a plane
Easy on the eyes
Evenly equalized
Effectively effortless
Efficient like Enterprise
Amazing abilities
Astonishing attributes
All thanks to Allah
Appreciative attitude
Unbearingly uncommon
Utterly unusual
Ultra comprehending
Understands what is confusing you
True Talent
Too blessed to break down
Tried and triumphant
Too tough to take down
Indefiably intriguing
Interesting incentives
Imperishable inner beauty
Impressive initiative
Fine, fair and favored
Far from foolish
Full of fulfillment
Found to be fluent
Underestimated and she's still unphased
Undefeated because she's so unplagued
Lovingly livacious
Laughing while living life
Lusted upon by lurkers

But lead by the Lord's light
Letting her light shine
And she shines so bright

She's an oxymoron
Good and bad to the sight

You ain't gotta ask me
What I'm trying to…
Spell
Baby it's you ooh ooh
B-E-A
U –
T-I-F
U- ooh ooh
-L
Beautiful

You ain't gotta ask me
What I'm trying to…
Spell
Baby it's you ooh ooh
B-E-A-
U –
T-I-F
U -
L
Beautiful.

Untitled (for Candy, 2) | *Billy Tuggle*

Two arms are walls that support me
Voice is sidewalk echo, radiator pop, floor creek,
Saturday morning radio
Kitchen-arena; bedroom-garden
Embrace circulates electricity
I return to this because it is mine
This house I belong to
This love, this dwelling is you

Placing lyric at the front of surrounding brains
Between road trips
Trying not to trip on this job's steps upward
The faith that powers this vehicle is the return
Prayers that the going-away, tossing words under spotlight
Reinforces our foundation

A Black One | *Kwabena Nixon*

here sistas
here mothers
here women
my words from me to you
I bow my head to you
cuz you bowed yo head for me
you bled for me, you fed me
you restored dignity
when we waz stored on the bottom of the ship
you breast-fed me, after master children took yo milk
we not lactose intolerant, it just was none left
so we did without
without you, we be still in the fields
but you dark daughter of Diaspora
you
kissed us when they said r lips
were too big and we gained confidence
we walked with a swagger for you
cause you walked with a rhythm for us
and we know no matter what that white man did
he couldn't move to the music we made
in bed
a maid, house keeper, cook, a maid
we watched and wept when beautiful Billie Holliday
played a maid
that made us want to be educated
read books and write r names and
make a better way for r families
and when we stole away from responsiblility
you wore pants and shoes and boxing gloves
tough love, cuz
you took punches, never turning the other cheek
you gave us creativity and poetry you told us
that r natural hair was cool and you gave us a
straighten comb, an afro pick
and even when we picked…the other side
becuz u a woman, becuz you know black woman magic

from yo black hips, from yo black thighs,
from yo black lips you gave us sips of black girl juice, mixed with
black girl scent and black girl sweat
so we might find r way back home
r way back home
and yes we gave you a rib, but you gave us a backbone
and a reason to live.

Meant | *King Gandy El*

I mean...

Mean I told her, "I love you." and I meant it.
Just not the way she imagined it when she listened.

She heard it like,
I'm here for you and cherish you enough to marriage you
We'll have 3 children, a house, picket fence and baby carriage too
When cats run up on me trying to holla I won't embarrass you

I meant it like,
May I have this dance, can I be yo friend, can I get in those pants?
What you doing after school
You should come through
I gotta pole in my basement
I'm just kidding like Jason...unless you gonna do it

She was acting like,
If you running low on dough, I'll have you smelling food
Like, if my dough is low, I'll cook my parent's food
If someone bothers me, I'm telling you
If my itch needs a scratch, I'll be next to you

What I look like turning down an offer that I can't refuse?

In all that, I had a goal. A goal that wasn't as precious as what I was taught to appreciate. Yes, I enjoyed the chase and the intimacy, but what I valued most was the love. I played it cool and grew to love her beyond my wildest dreams.
I learned how to woo a women by watching TV and that could never suffice in the long term so I had to turn to what my grandmother and mother taught me...

Love...
Black Love
        I told her "I love you."

                              And I meant it...

CONTRIBUTORS

Born in Maywood and raised in Peoria, Illinois, **Brandon Alexander Williams** is a poet, MC and DJ. He is the most recent recipient of the Grant Wood Fellowship and is a visiting instructor at the University of Iowa's School of Music where he teaches courses in Hip-Hop. Williams is an alumnus of Southern Illinois University-Carbondale where he produced "The Yard: An A'Capella/Hip-Hop Musical". As an active MC and DJ, he has performed and taught throughout the country, produced eight albums, published two books and given several guest lectures and keynotes centered around art-integrated education.

Featured as one of Los Angeles's highest-rated photographers!, Brian Freeman has been featured by *Under Armour, Mazda, USA Today, The Washington Post, Essence Magazine, Ebony Magazine, Washington Wizards, and STNDRD Magazine*. Brian studied Architecture at Hampton University and has years of experience in commercial and lifestyle photography. His innate ability to capture the soul of a moment and make timeless moments through photography has placed him in a league of extraordinary professional photographers.

A.D. Carson is a performance artist and educator from Decatur, Illinois. He received a Ph.D. in Rhetorics, Communication, and Information Design at Clemson University doing work that focuses on race, literature, history, and rhetorical performances. A 2016 recipient of the Martin Luther King, Jr. Award for Excellence in Service at Clemson, Carson worked with students, staff, faculty, and community members to raise awareness of historic, entrenched racism at the university through his See the Stripes campaign, which takes its name from his 2014 poem. His dissertation, "Owning My Masters: The Rhetorics of Rhymes & Revolutions," is a digital archive that features a 34 track rap album and was recognized by the Graduate Student Government as the 2017 Outstanding Dissertation. Carson is an award-winning artist with essays, music, and poetry published at a variety of diverse venues such as *The Guardian, Quiddity International Literary Journal and Public-Radio Program*, and *Journal for Cultural and Religious Theory*, among others. His essay "Trimalchio from Chicago: Flashing Lights and the Great Kanye in West Egg" appears in *The Cultural Impact of Kanye West* (Palgrave Macmillan, 2014), and "Oedipus—Not So Complex: A Blueprint for Literary Education" is in *Jay-Z: Essays on Hip Hop's Philosopher King* (McFarland & Co., 2011). Carson has written a novel, *COLD*, which hybridizes poetry, rap lyrics, and prose, and *The City: [un]poems, thoughts, rhymes & miscellany*, a collection of poems, short stories, and essays. Carson is currently assistant professor in Hip-Hop and the Global South at the University of Virginia. Follow A.D. Carson on Twitter/IG **@aydeethegreat.**

Ace Metaphor. Poet, Motivational speaker, Hopeless romantic. Over 500k online followers and 80 million online views. Co-founder of Metaphorically speaking, a Dayton based production company. Tours across the over as part of Ace Metaphor Productions

Adán Bean is an accomplished emcee, spoken word poet and voice-over actor hailing from the small town of Massillon, OH, but has called Atlanta home for almost 10 years. As one half of the retro-progressive hip hop group, The Remnant, Adán has released 3 projects with the band as well as toured the country extensively bringing the music to the masses. In addition to writing, recording and performing music, he co-runs the website ForthDistrict.com which focuses on art, music and conscious culture. Finally, as an SEM copywriter by day, Adán Bean can be found on stages across the country sharing his prose and poetry.

Add-2 has released several critically acclaimed projects such as "Save.Our.Souls", "More Missed Calls", "Between Heaven And Hell" and "Prey For The Poor". In 2016 he created Haven Studio which is a free music mentoring program that gives teens on the southside of Chicago a positive outlet to express themselves creatively. His music program has been featured on The Steve Harvey Show, Windy City Live, DNAInfo and more. Add-2 continues to use his voice and his platform to change the world around him.

Allah's Apprentice is a servant...that will give you bars as a lyricist and musician. Born and raised in Macon, GA, he is an emcee and trumpet player that is redefining music with sophisticated soul. Legend has it he can freestyle about anything and has never been seen without a trumpet.

Antwan André Patton (born February 1, 1975), better known by his stage name **Big Boi**, is an American rapper, songwriter, actor and record producer, best known for being a member of American **hip hop** duo **Outkast** alongside **André 3000**. His work in the duo has produced six studio albums. Big Boi's solo debut *Sir Lucious Left Foot: The Son of Chicco Dusty* was released in July 2010 to respectable sales and critical acclaim. He released his second studio album, ***Vicious Lies and Dangerous Rumors*** in 2012. Recently, the seven-time GRAMMY® Award-winning, RIAA diamond-certified musician released his celebrated third full-length solo album, *BOOMIVERSE*.

Billy Tuggle is a performance poet, slam champion, workshop facilitator, and event producer, having authored 2 poetry collections. He has been anthologized by publishers such as Write Bloody Publishing, Red Bench Press and Thoughtcrime Press. Billy was the 2015 National Head-to-Head Haiku Champion.

http://artistecard.com.BillyTuggle
www.facebook.com/backpackfiles

The Tony, Peabody & Emmy Award winning, 6-time HBO and Broadway Def Poet, **Black Ice** is credited with being a major pioneer of this millennium, turning spoken word into a mainstream art form.

With influences from Prince and J Dilla to Radiohead and fusion-era Miles Davis, St. Louis MC/producer/vocalist, **Blvck Spvde** clearly is not the pop-rap of fellow Gateway City natives. His musical palette -- warm and trippy synths, gritty hip-hop beats, and falsetto-infused, downtempo neo-soul -- is more in tune with the left-field soul/funk scenes of underground Detroit and L.A. Born and bred in St. Louis, MO, Spade (real name Veto Lamar Money) developed into a skilled artist performing as part of local indie rap/soul collective *Soul Tyde*, which originally formed in 1998. Their first, and only, album, *Hip-Hop & Soulful...Ish*, sold just a few hundred copies upon its release in 2003. While establishing himself as a solo artist, Spade was discovered by an A&R from the down-tempo/deep house-focused label *Om Records* at a performance in the California Bay Area in 2004. By 2007, the multi-threat soulster was signed to Om and issued the digital four-song EP, *Loves Right Here*, later that year. His debut full-length with the label, *To Serve With Love*, appeared shortly thereafter in 2008.

Brandon Douglas, a poet/emcee/actor/teaching artist/young black man native to Washington DC who uses his art selfishly and selflessly at the same time. Selfish because he uses art to vent and explore personal issues; Selfless because he uses art to share his knowledge and experience as a human being for others to learn from and use. He also believes that everyone has greatness to offer.

Chris James is a TED Talk speaker, national award winning poet and teaching artist who integrates art into education in public schools across America. He is an author of books *Black Boys Blues* and *The Odds Against US* and playwright of *DEAR BLACK PEOPLE*. Chris is the founder of Arkansas' staple gallery and poetry venue, *The House of Art*. As a success coach, Chris focuses on helping creative entrepreneurs to make a living off of their craft.

Born in Dayton, Ohio, **Chris Wiley** is a poet, writer, actor and Fine Arts graduate of The University of Cincinnati. He is also the creator and host of "Poetry In Motion-Dayton".

Corey Black is a St. Louis born poet, spoken word artist and host/creator of *Poetic Justice Open Mic*, St. Louis' biggest open mic night. He is a United States Marine Corps veteran and advocate for veterans battling PTSD and depression. Black believes that the art of spoken word has healing principles. His anthology *"Shoot The Messenger"* was released November of 2014.

Steve **"Cya"** Carter is a master of the arts, may it be visual, or poetically. Since the age of seven, he has been crafting song lyrics, and still active at the now age of 36. As an Advertising and Design major, he also gives his creative input to painting, drawing, layout, as well as graphic design. Steve uses this ability, as a platform to create awareness, politically, or to solve or improve upon a current design need. In his spare time, he likes to spend time with his friends who double as crew members of his car club, making music, gaming, or engulfing himself in sports.

Born in South-side Chicago, **Cyrus Speaks** is a traveling spoken word artist and minister, now based out of Atlanta, GA. Most notably, he's been a feature artist for P4CM (Passion for Christ Movement). While serving as a United States Marine, he noticed that mental and emotional oppression are just as devastating to people's lives as any war. This led him to educate and console through his spiritually charged poems. Whether he's performing at colleges, churches, corporate parties, or small clubs; Cyrus hopes that the words he speak don't just impress your ears, but that God uses them to impact your life.

Daunte Henderson is an author , educator and founder of the MADEMAN Foundation. Brother Henderson is passionate about changing the narrative of Black men through mentorship, writing and exposure. Follow his IG "@brotherhenderson" and Facebook fan page for more updates.

Dometi Pongo is an emcee at heart, curator by instinct and broadcast journalist by trade. His music explores the intersections of spirituality, self-reflection and social commentary. Born in Chicago to West African parents, Dometi adds global context to those conversations by leading annual cultural excursions to Ghana. In the States, he has curated award-winning arts exhibitions from the Twin Cities to Southern Illinois and Chicago that have elevated the work of poets, musicians, visual artists and authors. In broadcasting Dometi's 2015 feature chronicling the coverage of the Laquan McDonald shooting received finalist recognition for Best Radio Feature from the National Association of Black Journalists. Find music, podcasts, and other content at **www.dometipongo.com**

Drew Anderson (aka "**Droopy the Broke Baller**") is a veteran educator turned teaching artist and motivational speaker from New Orleans, LA. He is the founder and co-host of *Spit Dat* (the longest-running open mic in Washington DC) and creator of *C.R.U.N.K.* Academy which focuses on making learning fun for students through parody, poetry, hip hop, theatre and comedy. You can find out more about him at www.brokeballer.com.

Dion Jones, known creatively as **Dion Jetson**, is a writer, creator and overall creative from Chicago. Dion is the artist behind internationally released music projects: *The Ear & The Heart* and *Long Boys* that can be found on Apple Music, Spotify and Tidal. He is also the host of *The No 4Play Show* podcast which can be found on iTunes and iHeartRadio. Dion is an avid champion of black women, black love and all things black.| *DionJetson.com* | *TheNo4PlayShow.com*

Drunken Monkeee has been considered to be one of Chicago's most influential performance artists to come out of the Midwest because of his live shows, high energy personality, and out-of-the-box approach to art.

Bro. Tim **"El Thought"** Anderson-El is a father, community leader, poet, and spiritual advocate for youth in the St. Louis community. He has been married to his wife for six years and is a father to four children; this adds to his involvement in his community because he knows he is helping to shape the future for his children and grandchildren.

Frankiem Nicoli is Wisconsin born and Chicago raised; he is a 'from the heart writer'. Each performance will make you feel. Cultured by the likes of Real T@lk and K Love, Frankiem is one of the most vulnerable and skilled writers to be bred from Chicago.

George Jackson III, also known by his production alias *Authentik Made*, is a well traveled artist who has shared stages with such musical greats at Quincy Jones, MC Lyte, Leon Timbo, Jacob Collier, Eric Benet, Lee England Jr, Melanie Fiona, Robin Thicke and others. This Chicago bred artist plays 8 instruments and counting and is very versatile in his music style it ranges from Hip Hop, Soul, Country, R and B and Gospel/ Contemporary. He is a husband and father of three.

Harold Branch III who is affectionately known as "**HB**" is a Phoenix based speaker, trainer, entrepreneur and poet. HB hails from the Westside of Chicago, an area hard pressed and recognized as being one of the toughest and most oppressed neighborhoods in America. Despite being separated from his father when he was one and losing his mother to suicide at the age of two, he defied all odds and went on to become an applauded poet, speaker, and business trainer.

Primarily a poet, **Harold Green III** is an ever-evolving artist with a skill set that defies categorization. His vibrant storytelling and passionate lyrical delivery continue to captivate audiences both domestically and internationally. With repeat sell-out shows at some of Chicago's largest and most popular music venues, Green is not only a highly sought-after talent, but an equally respected band leader and event producer. He is the architect and curator of "Flowers for the Living", an annual collaboration project with some of the best singers and musicians Chicago has to offer. He is a proud son, brother, husband, father, teacher, coach and mentor. He is a visionary, leader, motivator and an overwhelmingly undeniable human being.

Native Chicagoan, **J. Ivy** is an award-winning performance poet, artist, author, song writer, actor, voice-over talent and motivational speaker. His work has earned him a *Peabody, Clio, Telly*, and *NAACP Image Award* and he is widely known for being the poet featured on Kanye West's Grammy-winning album *"The College Dropout,"* on the classic song *"Never Let Me Down,"* along with hip-hop icon Jay-Z. Due to his patented breath taking performances, J. Ivy was featured on three seasons of *HBO's Russell Simmons' Def Poetry*, two full seasons of *NBC's Sunday Night Football* and he is currently touring with his latest book/audio book and album, *"Dear Father: Breaking the Cycle of Pain"*.

J.C. Cowan born in Fort Polk, Louisiana as an army brat. Spending the majority of his childhood in Germany he was exposed to Hip Hop in 1979 and so began his love for writing. Entering the military right out of High School he continued to travel the world. After serving 8 years in the Army and serving in the Gulf War he settled in Charlotte N.C. in 2000 and began to spearhead the Spoken Word movement that still thrives till this day.

Jason Williams is a 39 year old poet, author, and public speaker that has graced stages, and open mics world wide. He Discovered a passion for writing at a very early age and is still one of the most dynamic poets of this generation. His unique style of creative passion combined with an unmatched delivery has separated him from the pack, and continues to open doors for his creative genius.

John the Author is a rapper, entrepreneur & activist who is pioneering a new way of doing things on the Chicago music scene. **John** once stated that the best kind of music an artist can create encourages a listener to think critically and live progressively. His ideas have proven to resonate as **John** is the founder of **BLACKENOMICS**, a quickly evolving movement & t-shirt line that brings awareness to the need for financial literacy education & black wealth building in underprivileged communities through the practice of group economics.

Jus Cuz, your favorite producer's favorite producer Overhyped and underrated, Jus Cuz's emotional production style makes for a unique listening experience. The Chicago South-sider has a very rare ability to combine multiple genres to fit into any pocket for any artist while still able to maintain a signature sound. A rare occurrence amongst many producers in this current era. Jus Cuz's self-branded, Band New Old School style is definitely one worth getting familiar with, as he grows & matures as a phenomenal producer as well as an artist.

Just Flo is a Motivational, Hip Hop Artist & Speed Painter from the South Side of Chicago. & from the very start, My Love & Heart, has belonged to Music and Art! He specializes in: Poetry, Rap, Singing, Live Artistry, Comedy Improv, Illustration, Murals & Tattoos. His goal is to Create Harmony & Cultivate Healing within my Family, Community & throughout the World!

Educator, poet, motivational speaker and activist, **Karega Bailey**, a native of Sacramento, California is a successful product of collective contributions from the Sacramento community. Mentoring services of The 100 Black Men of America, Inc (*Sacramento*) and the family services offered by the Center for Fathers & Families provided Mr. Bailey with the support and direction needed to succeed amidst the socioeconomic stressors. After becoming a proud alumni of Hampton University, he acquired over nine years in Special Education and School Leadership, fostering resiliency and hope through Spoken Word and Hip Hop. Mr. Bailey is currently *Dean of Culture and Climate* at *Roses in Concrete Community School* in Oakland, CA.

King Gandy El is a media pluralist with vision and compassion.

Keith Rodgers was born and raised in Lake Hamilton, Florida (Polk County). U.S. Veteran, entrepreneur, poet, author, campaign manager, promoter, comedian, host, activist, creative writing workshop facilitator, consultant and father of two daughters! The Founder and CEO of *Black On Black Rhyme* and *The BackTalk Poetry Troupe*, host of *Tallahassee Nights Live*!, creator of "staccatos" which are short poems, sayings or words that have a total different meaning once the statement is read after saying the word! One of the wittiest people you will ever meet!

Kwabena Antoine Nixon is an author, poet and speaker, born on the west side of Chicago. He is the founder of *Be Inspired Works*.

kwabena foli was born in Belgium and raised in the Southside of Chicago. He is a former Chicago poetry slam champion and national poetry slam finalist. Transitioning from the stage to the page in 2015, kwabena began sharing his writings via social media --many of which becoming viral with over 14 million shares since. His content has appeared on cultural platforms such as All Def Poetry, forharriet, MadameNoire, blkcreatives and others. His work is also anthologized in Revise the Psalm: Work Celebrating the Writing of Gwendolyn Brooks from Curbside press. In June of 2017, kwabena foli published *learning rhythm* via *Flowered Concrete press* that quickly reached the top 100 of poetry from an African American writer on Amazon, and the top 10 of African art on Kindle.

PVTSTCK emcee/producer, **L.A. VanGogh** is a multitalented man from Dolton, IL. His musical style is thought provoking and playful. The content is earnest, dealing with personal, in-depth subject matters with a soulful and meditative groove.

LaRoyce Hawkins is an actor, stand-up comic, spoken word artist, and musician. Hawkins stars on NBC's police drama *Chicago P.D.*, where he portrays Officer Kevin Atwater. The show is in its fifth season. Hawkins also has a minor recurring role on the crossover show ***Chicago Fire***.

Lee England Jr. is an American violinist, vocalist, arranger, and composer from Waukegan, IL. He gained recognition in 2009 after his audition for MTV's Making The Band ***Making The Band*** impressed executive producer **Sean Combs** and landed him a spot on the show as the only "non-traditional" instrumentalist. Since then, he has been featured on shows like **Jimmy Kimmel Live** and **The Mo'Nique Show**, and has shared the stage with musicians like Stevie Wonder, Beyoncé, and Jay-Z. In 2010, England performed at a private party for **Michael Jordan**. Jordan was so impressed with England's abilities that he offered him an endorsement deal with his shoe brand. Most recently, England performed at the **Geffen Playhouse** and attracted the attention of legendary music producer, Quincy Jones; he was subsequently signed to Jones's management company: Quincy Jones Productions.

Born and raised on the Southeast side of Chicago, Limitless Soundz offers what he calls "Pan-African Trap Solution Rap" music where he fuses the ideologies of Marcus Garvey, Malcolm X, and Huey P. Newton with trap music. With the common themes of self sufficiency, healthy eating and African Spirituality, Limitless strives to provide sound solutions to the problems faced by African descendants on a global scale. With music being his focal point, Limitless also shares his creativity as a songwriter, poet, host, motivational speaker, Rap Writing Instructor and a Columbia College graduate with a BA in Journalism.

Louis Conphliction isn't an entertainer, he is Entertainment! Whether ravaging sixteen bars, serenading love interests or igniting our innermost passions with poetry, you are bound to request Louis Conphliction's presence inside of your hearts, minds and homes. A native of St. Louis, he is heavily influenced by the culture of his city. Noticing a need for upliftment, he decides to use his talents to create a self-love and self-awareness centered movement, utilizing mentorship, eclectic beats and empowering words.

Malari Khan **SankofaWaters** AKA *Ugly Boy Modeling* is a writer, rapper, producer, director, and graphic designer with works focusing on race, politics, love, and ratchetness. He has featured on shows such as BET's Lyric Cafe and opened up for artists such as Raekwon, The Last Poets, and Lil B.

Though globally known for his television work, **Malcolm-Jamal Warner** is equally at home in the world of spoken word. While a heavy presence in the resurgence of the Los Angeles underground spoken word movement in the mid-90's, Warner formed Miles Long, a jazz funk spoken word band where he also plays electric and upright bass. He has performed on HBO's Def Poetry Jam, Lyric Cafe, Verses and Flow, and various jazz festivals. In 2015, Warner, along with Robert Glasper and Lalah Hathaway, won a Grammy Award for Best Traditional R&B performance for their cover of Stevie Wonder's "Jesus Children," a tribute to the children if Sandy Hook Elementary. All 3 of Warner's Cds can be found at **malcolmjamalwarner.com**.

Matt Simpson is a father, Community Development Strategist and Entrepreneur based in Rockford, Illinois. He is co-founder of the Wabongo Leadership Council, and managing partner of Eight Fifteen Capital, LLC. In addition to his entrepreneurial and community development efforts Simpson aspires to be a true Man of Culture, in the spirit of the great Aime Cesaire.

Mel Roberson (MelRob) is an accomplished actor, spoken word artist, Amazon best selling author and speaker, and successful entrepreneur. His entertainment style is the perfect balance of street sense and book smarts. Check him out at www.melroberson.com

Born & raised on Westside of Chicago Illinois, **Moementum** witnessed a lot of tragedy which inspired him to write. I've been writing for over 30 plus years & performing 16 years. I'm the Co-Founder of a poetry organization called 3BM (2003). I love God, I love LOVE & I love to speak life. I want to paint the world beautiful with words.

Born in **Takoma Park, MD** by the way of Jamaica, **Orville the Poet** is known for his charismatic, confident, goal driven mindset, and his passion for poetry. Using his pen to get him through life experiences, Orville uses his passion for the arts to raise awareness, speak vivid truths, and uplift his community.

Pages Matam is an international artist & educator from Cameroon, Central Africa, currently residing in Washington D.C. He is the *Director of Poetry Events* for *Busboys and Poets*, a *Callaloo Fellow*, and *Write Bloody* published author of *The Heart of a Comet (2014)*, which won Best New Book 2014 from *Beltway Poetry Quaterly* and was a Teaching for Change bestseller. A national and 2x regional poetry slam champion, he has passions in the field of education, violence and abuse trauma work, immigration reform and youth advocacy.

Phenom, (born Teh'Ray Hale), has dedicated his life to empowering the People through his music. In 1995, First Lady, Michelle Obama chose him for the Public Allies program where he had the opportunity to work with and teach youth about violence prevention strategies. As the Founder and CEO of the award-winning *P.O.E.T.R.E.E. Chicago* (People's Organized Entertainment Teaching Righteous Education Everywhere), Phenom was influenced to start *L.Y.R.I.C*, (Let Your Rhymes Inspire Creativity) with co-founder and national poet K-Love in 2009. Today, the L.Y.R.I.C program serves Chicago-based high school students and offers them opportunity to write and perform poetry as a non-violent means to stopping the violence in their neighborhoods. As a main member of Hip-Hop Detoxx, in the fall of 2017 Phenom traveled to Iraq as a cultural/ spiritual ambassador for Hip-Hop culture. His goal is to inspire change in the urban neighborhoods of Chi-town and abroad.

Pugs Atomz A stalwart and revered figure from the Chicago scene, Pugs Atomz is a trailblazer who laid the ground work for many artists in the area today. From mural art, music, video, radio (CTA Radio) to clothing design (Iridium Clothing Co/ USUWE) he pushes the culture. His most recent album is "Highly Irregular" with producer/Dj Mulatto Patriot.

Native to Chicago, **Que Billah** is an entertainer artist, director, donut expert, baker and designer.

Ques is a Chicago spoken word artist. Having forged a powerful reputation amongst his hometown, his work is the voice of the youth as he consistently writes on the issues that impact African-Americans. Spiritually writing like an old griot, Ques has a powerful voice and an intense stage presence that reverently honors the luminaries of the past with a fresh flavor all his own. His motive is to plant a seed of change and to remind audiences everywhere to NEVER FORGET.

Rage Almighty is spoken word artist/writer from Dallas TX by way of Boston MA. Some of his accolades I include 2017 Bayou City Champion, 2016 2nd place Individual World Poetry Slam winner & the United States representative in the World Poetry Cup Slam in Paris France.

"Rashad tha Poet" Rayford is an activist, actor and award winning poet/MC. He is poet mentor with Southern Word a non profit in Nashville that reaches over 10,000 young people a year in 7 counties. Rashad is a soul-hop artist specializing in jazz fused hip-hop. | **rashadthapoet.com**

Hailing from Rock Island, IL as featured in the Quad City Times, **John 'Rewind' Gunter**, Jr is a Quad City based spoken word, writer and hip-hop lyricist. A graduate of Illinois State University and Georgia State University he has generated a substantial following in the both the spoken word and hip-hop scene. He boasts a keen sense of realism paired with a catchy and melodic flow. Rewind is a loving father and husband and humanitarian, creator of the "Ay, Pops" blog and founder of Fresh Epidemics Entertainment. Rewind's focus is to bring FRESH thoughts with realistic images and he challenges others to lift as they climb."

Rodzilla is an internationally known spoken word impresario, carrying the torch lit long ago by ancestor griots and members of the Black Arts Movement. Heralded as the Blackademic this scholar represents the hip hop intellectual at its finest with his brand of edutainment... He has performed in every noteworthy poetry den in the US representing a special brand of lyricism called that NorthernCaliformulaSacramentoIzm, Rodzilla is one of the most unique poetic savants around.

With his hometown of Chicago on his back and the sounds of soul in his roots, Brooklyn-based emcee **R.O.E.** blends an urban vibe with poetic lyricism and music that hits straight to the heart that will attract anyone with an affection for alternative hip hop.

Sam Trump is a multi-instrumentalist/singer/ songwriter from Houston, TX, and has been a student of music from first picking up the trumpet at age 7. Since moving to Chicago in 2009 to obtain his fine arts degree in music, he has become heavily involved in Chicago's live music scene as a band leader, sideman, and show curator.

Chicago-based artist **Sean Ace**'s 2012 single "Ms. Natural," celebrated and championed women of natural hair from all over the globe - and was the first of its kind. The creator of "champion music," this hard-hitting hip-hop artist uses his witty and vivid lyrics over soulful beats for his music's backdrop, recalling stories of growing up on Chicago's south side along with empowering anthems for the people.

Named one of the "Top 6 STL Artists to Watch in 2016" by St. Louis Post Dispatch, **Steve N. Clair** is a hip hop recording artist half of the hip-hop duo, The Domino Effect along with being a professional Filmmaker & Photographer. He is also the founder/owner of independent film production company, Flyy Awayy Films.

Chicago native T. L. Williams is an iconic & award-winning singer-songwriter, producer, and actor. He is also the founder of Symphony Of Change, an arts organization dedicated to helping school band programs in America.

Tebe Zalango is a violinist, composer, singer, songwriter, rapper, and international spoken word artist. Tebe has traveled across the nation and to multiple countries with a message of awareness and love.

Find out more at **www.zalangomusic.com**.

The Boy Illinois hails from the southeast side of Chicago. He is an indie artist who just recently did a partnership with Priority Records.

Antonio "**Toni Mono**" Monix, is a Hip Hop spoken word artist from the south side of Chicago, IL. Mono's interest in poetry began nearly as long as he could write sentences, winning his first poetry contest in his 2nd grade classroom. At 19, Mono ran into an organization named L.Y.R.I.C. Mentoring that he joined and soon became a youth leader in the community; that heightened his passion for mentoring and provided a strong community artist platform for him. Currently Toni Mono is a teaching-artist with several organizations and is developing a word movement titled "Monoism" that delves into 'word understandings'.

Dayton native, **Tripp Fontane**, has been slowly but surely creating a name for himself. Coming from humble beginnings, Tripp uses his life experience to paint a very unique picture of his atmosphere and his upbringing. Making tactful use of transparency and vulnerability, no topic is off limits. His gritty content and smooth delivery have both made him a fan favorite. From community work to event coordinating, Tripp Fontane relentlessly uses his gifts to benefit the minds and everyday lives of the people. You're always in for a one of a kind poetry experience!

Born in Saginaw, MI, writer/spoken word artist **Truth B. Told** (Christopher Owens) has written for and appeared in a commercial for BET's "Black History Moment" vignettes and has opened for acts such as Mint Condition and Floetry. Truth B. Told received 2012 Spoken Word Album of the Year and 2013 Spoken Word Artist of the Year honors at the National Poetry Awards. Currently, he is completing his Masters in Creative Writing from Wilkes University with concentrations in poetry and fiction, as well as completing his first novel.

Tyson Langhorn was born and raised in Peoria, Illinois. His love for humanity was instilled in him since birth, being the youngest of four boys with a younger sister soon thereafter. He took a liking to exploring his lyrical talents early in life, but took a much more serious approach while furthering his education at Alcorn State University. Tyson is currently the father of three adorable girls and aspires to expand his artistic views thru a variety of entertainment platforms.

Yaw Agyeman is an interdisciplinary performing artist born in Chicago. He works primarily as a musician/sound designer but also has an extensive theater background (actor) and makes photos. Yaw's work addresses language as cultural currency. His work also uses space as a way to share music, community, and culture.

Authentic hip-hop, diverse style, unique delivery, and creative word play all describe recording artist, **Yusha Assad**. Born Joshua Blackwell, Yusha is a North Carolina native by way of Washington, DC, striving toward a future of success. Humbled by his roots, Yusha connects to the soul of his listeners while providing reflections of how one should follow their heart's and struggle/strive to reach their dreams.

Born in Leesville, Louisiana to a humble and disciplined family. **Zeaux Indigeaux's** greatest influences on his writing and who he is as a person are his heritage, southern upbringing, love for education, desire for social justice, hip hop, and comic books.

"Poetry has helped bring me through depression and anxiety since the first time I picked up a pen in 3rd grade. I can only hope to inspire others to find their passion as I indulge in my own."

13 of Nazareth is a poet from Virginia living with epilepsy. a dry sense of humor and peace of mind over everything. social media: @13ofnazareth | web adress: **13ofnazareth.net**

Made in the USA
San Bernardino, CA
15 January 2020